# DANCING IN THE OPERATING ROOM
# BY
# BRUCE C. DAVIS

# Also by Bruce C Davis

*Available on Amazon in print or most e-book formats*

*Thieves Profit*
*Glowgems for Profit*
*Initial Profit (short story)*
*That Which Is Human*
*Queen Mab Courtesy*

*For Jen & Chris
with love

Bruce*

Copyright 2015 by Bruce C Davis

All rights reserved under International and Panamerican Copyright Conventions. Published in the United States.

This work is autobiographical in nature. All events are true and accurate but names, timeframes and identifying circumstances may have been changed to protect patient anonymity. Where actual names are given, they are used with the knowledge and permission of the individuals named.

First Publication: March 2015

# DANCING IN THE OPERATING ROOM

Introduction: Why Bother?

I have sometimes been asked, "Why do you write this stuff? Why expose yourself like that?" in comments about some of my more personal essays.

A big reason is that it is therapeutic. A friend once commented on an essay, "A burden shared is a burden lightened." I write not so much to share a burden as to exorcise some demons through writing about them. If I write this stuff down and put it out there, it's no longer running around in my head making me crazy. Confession can be a powerful tool for healing.

The Wise Woman (my wife) tells me that owning too much, taking too much responsibility for things I can't control, is itself a form of arrogance and narcissism. She's right, but hyper-responsibility is a character trait of all surgeons. We must find ways to live with it. Writing about it helps me with that.

Finally, I write about this stuff to give others a glimpse of a world they will never see except on one of the worst days of their lives. It's a world that my colleagues and I inhabit every working day. I work with some of the most dedicated and intelligent people that I have ever known. Most of them could excel at any trade or profession they choose. They choose to work trauma. It is an honor to be associated with them.

What We Do

It's a rainy Saturday night, a welcome rarity in the Phoenix Valley. It's not the hard rain of the monsoons in August, but a light, steady winter rain. The Emergency Room has been fairly quiet and the trauma service has had no calls since change of shift twelve hours earlier. That is about to change.

The pagers don't all go off at once, but rather in a rolling wave from the trauma nurse to the lab tech to the x-ray tech and finally to the trauma surgeon. The small green screens all deliver the same message:

"Level one by ground, ETA 10 min, RED

"GSW to chest and abdomen, no vitals given"

The team gathers in ER bay 53, one of four trauma bays, all prestocked with equipment and supplies above and beyond the normal emergency room requirements. There are sterile instrument packs for central line insertion, chest tube trays, suture trays and an emergency thoracotomy pack. There are rapid infusers – IV pumps that can push fluids at rates of 250cc to 400cc per minute; pneumatic tourniquets; a cast cart with webbing and plaster; and the usual stock of sterile gloves, gauze, and suture.

The conversation is light, that of people who have worked together many times before greeting one another and bantering. A dark haired woman enters and moves to the head of the ER gurney that occupies the center of the bay. She is young, of medium height and build; attractive in spite of the almost shapeless surgical scrubs she wears and the lack of make-up. She would look nice in a short summer dress on the patio of a Scottsdale nightspot or strolling in La Condesa in Mexico City.

A few minutes later the ER clerk announces over the intercom, "Trauma is here in 53", and the light banter ceases. Eyes swing to the paramedics moving quickly but purposefully into the bay.

For the first time the dark haired woman speaks, "Go ahead with report," she says with a light Mexican Spanish accent.

One of the paramedics speaks out, "28 year old male shot twice, once in the left chest, entry just below the nipple, exit posterior near the tenth rib. Second wound enters in the left flank, exits in the right upper quadrant. Pressure has been low, in the 70's systolic; pulse 130. No breath sounds on the left. We started two IV's, 18 gauges in the right forearm and in the left antecubital. He's gotten 900cc of saline en route and 100 mikes of fentanyl."

"Thank you," says the dark haired woman, already pressing a stethoscope to the man's chest as a nurse wields surgical shears, cutting away his bloody clothing. Other techs move in attaching oximetry and EKG monitors, checking the integrity of the IV lines and removing his shoes and pants.

"I want to set up for a chest tube on the left and we'll need the O negative emergency blood," says the woman, clearly taking charge of the team. She glances at the monitors. "Better call the blood bank and start the massive transfusion protocol and tell the OR to set up for a laparotomy."

Rapidly but clearly she calls out the list of his wounds, his breath sounds, his other physical findings. She asks him if he has other medical issues; if he takes medications; if he has any drug allergies; all the while doing a quick head to toe exam.

She pulls on sterile gloves and sets out the instruments she will need to insert a drainage tube into the left side of the man's chest in order to drain blood and reinflate his collapsed lung.

A technician asks, "What size tube, Dr. C?"

The trauma surgeon, for that is who the dark haired woman with the slight Mexican accent is, answers, "34 French," without looking up from her work. She trusts the technician to get the right tube and have it ready by the time she has made a small incision in the patient's skin and probed through the muscle into the chest cavity. She inserts the tube and a rush of air and blood flows through it into a collection device. She secures the tube with a few quick sutures.

"Alright people, lets package him and move."

By this time, the rapid infusers have pumped almost 500cc of red blood cells, an equal volume of plasma, and a liter of saline into the man's veins. His blood pressure is better, although still low, and his heart rate has slowed, signs that the fluids have helped replace some of what he has lost.

The side rails of the gurney are raised and it starts to move, pushed by the trauma nurse who watches the electronic readout of his pulse and blood pressure on the small screen mounted by his feet.

Techs follow closely, pushing the IV poles and keeping the lines from becoming tangled.

Eighteen minutes after arrival, he reaches the operating room, a bit better than average but not a record. Twenty-three minutes after arrival and five after reaching the OR he has been anesthetized, scrubbed, and draped and the surgeon makes her first incision.

Two hours and forty-seven minutes later the incision is closed and the patient is being moved from the OR table to an ICU bed. He will remain intubated and on a ventilator for the rest of the night. The bullet tore off a piece of his left kidney, lacerated his pancreas, shredded his splenic artery and punched through his stomach and liver before exiting the front of his abdomen.

In a single operation, the trauma surgeon over sewed the bleeding upper pole of the patient's kidney, took out his spleen, removed the tail of his pancreas, removed a short segment of small intestine and put the ends back together, closed two holes in his stomach and cauterized bleeding areas in his liver. She placed drains in the area and closed her incision.

She follows the gurney to the elevator for the short ride up one floor to the surgical intensive care unit. She gives orders for his ventilator settings, his IV fluids, antibiotics, and mundane things such as dressing and drain care. Over the next twelve hours she will monitor his oxygen levels and vital signs, adjust fluids and ventilator settings, check on his urine output and review his morning x-rays.

Three days later, he is leaking bile from one of his drains, a potential sign of an intestinal leak. She takes him back to surgery and explores the abdomen. The bile is leaking from the liver wound. The intestine is intact and the bile leak is fixed with a single stitch.

His recovery is slow – his lung doesn't seal right away, his intestine shuts down for almost a week before opening up, he leaks pancreatic fluid from his drain – but he survives and goes home twenty days after being shot.

This is a summary of an actual case handled by one of my colleagues. It is unusual only because penetrating trauma is unusual in my trauma center, accounting for just twelve percent of all admissions. What is common to all of the injuries we handle is the team approach with the trauma surgeon as the team leader. Also key is the ability of that surgeon to handle a wide variety of surgical problems across multiple specialties – in this case, a kidney repair, a splenectomy, a partial pancreatectomy, repair of stomach and intestine, repair of the liver, ventilator management, critical care management, antibiotic selection, wound management and discharge planning.

Trauma surgery mixes general surgery at its best with critical care medicine. It requires a good grounding in orthopedics, neurosurgery, plastic surgery, chest and vascular surgery, and emergency medicine. Even if you aren't going to be the one actually operating on a complex fracture or a brain hemorrhage, you need to know what you are looking at and understand the principals of managing those problems so that you can communicate effectively with the consultants you call. You never know what's going to come through the ER door on any given day.

## The Dance

I don't dance. I have no rhythm and a tin ear. My attempts at dance, usually fueled by alcohol, amount to rocking back and forth or flailing about as if having some sort of bizarre seizure.

So it's ironic that I married a classically trained dancer who realized after high school that she did not have the body to be a prima ballerina and decided to go to nursing school. Nevertheless, she regularly took master's classes with the American Ballet Theater during time she was in college at Georgetown. For her, trying to dance with me is an exercise in saintly patience combined with steel-toed shoes.

It's different in the operating room. She has been my first assistant for twenty years and when we operate together, it's as close to dancing together as we will ever get. There is a rhythm to surgery, a practiced flow of movement and action not unlike a dance. When two people have worked together for a long time, they learn to anticipate each other's moves and respond without cues or conversation, just like practiced dance partners. It's actually harder for a surgeon to be a good assistant than for a nurse or technician. Surgeons tend to want to control the operation and forget their job is to make the operating surgeon look good. It's like both partners in a dance trying to lead at the same time. A good assistant, like a good dance partner, knows when to lead, when to follow, and how to make the dance flow smoothly. They can't make a poor surgeon look good, but they can make a good surgeon look great.

If the operation is a dance, the circulating nurse, the scrub tech and the anesthesiologist are the orchestra. They provide the essential accompaniment to the partners at the table. The dancers could not function without them. If the orchestra is off by even half a beat, the flow and form of the dance falter.

I have often felt this strange symphony of motion in the operating room with a good assistant. Athletes refer to it as being 'in the zone', and I suppose skilled practitioners in any field have a similar experience.

My wife and I dance well together in surgery, in part because we have always been on the same wavelength and in part because she has a natural understanding of physical movement. Her dance experience has given her a grace and economy of motion that never fail to excite and impress me. There is no one I'd rather have with me on a complex robotic or laparoscopic case. Dancing in the OR is a form of intimacy as intense as any on the ballroom floor.

Going Home

She's 17 years old and going home tomorrow. Today we are working with Social Service and Case Management to get all the equipment she and her family will need for her ongoing care – dressing supplies, a walker, crutches, a wheelchair and a raised commode seat.

She's 17 years old and three weeks ago I amputated her right leg above the knee. Before that operation she went through six surgeries to try to salvage the leg.

She's just an ordinary kid. Not a star athlete, not a great student. She likes horses and Harry Potter and boating with family and friends on Lake Saguaro. She wonders if she'll be able to graduate from high school this year, if she'll ever be able to swim again, if she will be able to work as a hairdresser, which was her goal after graduation.

It was a weekend night full of fun and a few really bad decisions. Underage drinking, driving too fast on the 101 and a fight with her boyfriend all played a part. I wasn't on when she came in, but was involved in her care as the rounding surgeon for the trauma service off and on for the whole six weeks she was in the hospital.

Her right leg got caught on something under the dashboard when the car rolled. Her boyfriend, who was driving, was ejected and died at the scene. Her right knee was dislocated posteriorly and the tibia and fibula, the two bones of the lower leg were shattered. Most of the skin on the lower part of her leg was degloved, ripped off of the underlying muscle. There was serious talk between the orthopedic surgeon and the trauma surgeon of completing the amputation that night. But she was 17 years old and healthy. Instead they went to surgery and did what they could.

Posterior knee dislocations are particularly devastating injuries because of the high incidence of injury to the popliteal artery. It's the blood supply to everything below the knee and is runs through a narrow space right behind the lower end of the femur and upper end of the tibia. It's relatively fixed in place by the big muscle groups around the joint and so when the tibia moves backwards in a posterior dislocation it can shear the vessel in two just like a guillotine.

The first goal in a vascular injury like this is to stabilize the bones. The leg will tolerate up to four hours of warm ischemia time, longer if the tissue is chilled, but vascular repairs are sensitive and don't tolerate twisting, kinking or tension. If the bones aren't secured, any repair will fail.

Popliteal arteries are hard to get at. Direct repair is rarely possible. More commonly a piece of vein is harvested and used to jump across the damaged segment from good vessel above to good vessel below.

In this case, there wasn't much good vessel above or below. The artery hadn't been sheared cleanly but rather had been stretched until it ripped. That caused unseen damage to the intima, the lining of the vessel, for a considerable distance above the visible tear. The degloving had also disrupted the vessels below the knee so there wasn't much to jump a graft to down there.

The orthopedic surgeon put on an external fixator, an erector set like device of rods and pins that screw into the bone and attach to a lightweight external frame that keeps the bone from moving. The vascular surgeon did a vein graft and the trauma surgeon pulled what skin he could over the open wound. A vacuum dressing completed the first procedure.

I saw her on ICU rounds a few hours later and knew she was in trouble. Her blood was still acidotic, too much lactic acid in circulation, a sign of tissue that wasn't getting enough oxygen. There was no detectable pulse below the knee and her toes were purple. The vascular surgeon took her back to surgery an hour later, and again six hours after that. And again. And again. All the time moving his graft to different tiny vessels in the lower leg looking for one that would support enough flow to nourish the muscles. One by one they shut down and the muscles died. After 18 days in the ICU on multiple antibiotics, sodium bicarbonate to correct the acidosis and heparin to keep the vessels from clotting off, we had the difficult conversation with her and her family.

She's going home tomorrow.

First Death

They say you never forget your first patient death. That wasn't true for me. I had been present at several deaths before the first one that I truly remember. I started my first clinical clerkships late in my second year of medical school at an inner city hospital. I was present for several ER and ICU deaths within my first few days on the Medicine service. They were nameless old people for me. I had examined them on rounds with the rest of the circus of students and residents, but hadn't really connected with them except as clinical exercises.

That wasn't the case with Anya. She was a bit older than I, almost thirty. She wasn't classically beautiful, but had a pale-skinned, ethereal look that captivated me. She came into the hospital complaining of progressive shortness of breath. She was faintly amused at my earnest but clumsy physical exam and the endlessly detailed medical history I dutifully recorded. I listened to her lungs and percussed her chest and documented the diminished breath sounds on the left, the dullness to percussion, and the asymmetry of her chest expansion when she took a deep breath. All signs of a pleural effusion, a collection of fluid in the chest between the lung and the chest wall.

The pleural space isn't usually a space at all. Rather it's a pair of slick membranes wrapping around the lung and the inner surface of the chest wall that allow the lung to move smoothly in and out as the chest expands and contracts. The lung itself is basically a big balloon, or more accurately, a cluster of thousands and thousands of tiny balloons held together by blood vessels and tiny air tubes called bronchioles. Unsupported, the lung will collapse under its own weight. What keeps it expanded is a vacuum in the pleural space. When we breathe in, the expanding chest pulls the lung outward causing it to fill with air, then collapses it as the chest wall moves inward when we breath out.

Anything that gets into that potential space between the lung and the chest wall disrupts the vacuum and disturbs the mechanics of breathing. Air can do this, whether from a hole in the lung or a hole in the chest, which allows air in from the outside. This is called a pneumothorax and is commonly seen in trauma. An effusion is fluid in the same space. Effusions may have many causes ranging from trauma to infection to malignancy and the treatment is based largely on the cause.

Anya's effusion seemed puzzling to me, at least as a medical student, since she was a slim, athletic young woman who said she enjoyed running, bicycling and rock climbing. I was accustomed to thinking of effusions as being due to heart failure or malnutrition or pneumonia, none of which seemed to apply here.

I stammered something to her about talking things over with my resident and asked if she needed the nurse. She smiled and said she was fine and hoped I'd be back soon with some word about what we would do next.

I presented her history and physical to my resident and he asked if there had been any x-rays taken. There was just a chest x-ray. He opened her chart and ordered a mammogram, an upper GI series and a barium enema. Thoroughly confused, I asked why.

"She's got cancer," he said. "Come on. You're going to do your first thoracentesis."

I followed him back to her room, He spent a few minutes reviewing with her the history I'd taken and then asked if he could reexamine her breasts. She nodded and he did a much more extensive exam than the shy, cursory one I had done.

"Did you notice the asymmetry?" he asked me, indicating the difference in size of the breasts. I had, but didn't know what to make of it. I knew from my reading that there is often a distinct difference in size between right and left breasts in some women and that it didn't necessarily indicate pathology.

"Has your left breast always been a bit larger?" He asked her. No, she said, the left had grown notably over the past six months.

The nurse brought in a tray of instruments and a liter sized glass bottle with a tight rubber stopper sealed to the top.

The resident walked me through the thoracentesis – drainage of the chest with a long needle. Under some local anesthesia, a large bore needle is directed through the skin and muscle between the ribs in the middle of the back. Anya bore up stoically and when I got bloody fluid back, I was alarmed.

The resident said, "Good. Now connect the tubing to the needle and plug the other end into the bottle."

I did as he directed and found that the bottle was a vacuum container, like a giant blood draw tube. Soon, we had a liter of fluid in the bottle. The nurse switched the bottle for another one and we drew off another 800cc before the flow stopped. By that time, Anya was breathing noticeably better. She thanked me.

I removed the needle from her chest and applied a gauze pad. The nurse took the bottles and called for a lab pick-up.

Outside in the hallway, the resident said, "She probably has a diffuse breast cancer. That's why her left breast is larger. There is no mass. Most of the breast is replaced by the tumor. It's easy to miss if you don't notice the difference in hardness between the two sides." Her left breast was larger and I had noticed that it was firmer than the right.

The next day, the surgeons saw her and scheduled her for a breast biopsy and possible mastectomy. The fluid analysis showed "malignant, poorly differentiated cells, consistent with breast primary"

She came back from surgery in the evening, minus her left breast. I went to see her before I went home for the night. I was stunned, but she was calm. I had little to offer her in the way of information or wisdom, but she talked with me for a while about her parents and her cat. She asked if I had family and if they were in Chicago. It seemed surreal. We were having a normal conversation, as if we had met at a social function and were getting to know each other. I think I fell in love with her a little bit.

I saw her off and on over the next six weeks as she was in and out of the clinic and hospital getting chemotherapy. Chemo in those days was less effective and more toxic than the agents we use today. I stayed with her a couple of times after evening rounds as she battled waves of nausea. We never touched, other than in a clinical way, and our conversations were casual. I don't know how she felt about me. I suspect she thought of me as a kind of younger brother, or maybe a stray puppy she had picked up. I desperately wanted her to get better and be well again.

About three months after her initial diagnosis she came back to the emergency room with another effusion. I had moved on to my Pediatrics rotation and was in the outpatient clinic seeing runny noses and rashes when the Chief Resident found me.

"Dr. P from oncology is looking for you," she said. "There's a patient asking for you." She gave Anya's name. "Is she a relative?"

"No," I said. "Just a patient I saw on my last rotation."

She looked a little dubious. Patients didn't ask for medical students by name. She told me to finish with the child I was currently seeing, and then go find Dr. P.

I did and the oncologist seemed to understand Anya's request. He directed me to her hospital room.

She looked terrible. She was skeletally thin and gasping for breath despite the tube in her chest that drained reddish fluid into a complex of suction bottles at her bedside.

She smiled when she saw me and said, "I didn't want to go without saying goodbye."

"Are they transferring you to another hospital?" I asked and then wished I could take it back.

She just smiled again, shook her head, and closed her eyes. I sat with her as she slept. About three in the morning, she stopped breathing and was gone.

High C

She is twenty-five and referred for evaluation of a thyroid nodule. As is often the case, this one was found incidentally when she had a sore throat. An astute primary care doctor thought she felt a mass and got an ultrasound. The nodule measured 2.3 cm and so by the accepted protocol for thyroid lumps, an ultrasound guided fine needle aspiration (FNA) was done. (A fine needle is used to suck up some cells from the mass and send them to pathology for analysis.)

Most thyroid nodules are benign – about 85%. But 15% are malignant and those are heavily skewed toward young women. The bulk of thyroid cancers fall into one of two categories: Papillary cancers are most common and are distinctive on FNA; Follicular cancers are less well defined and difficult to distinguish from benign follicular adenomas on FNA. Generally a finding of a follicular lesion on FNA of the thyroid leads to a thyroid lobectomy – removing the half of the gland where the tumor lives.

Her FNA showed a 'follicular nodule of indeterminate nature'. In other words, the pathologist can't tell me whether it is benign or malignant based on the needle aspiration. At her age, her risk of this being malignant is as high as thirty percent.

I sit down and talk with her about surgery. She listens as I outline the operation and it's purpose. I tell her about the small risk of injury to her recurrent laryngeal nerves. They are the nerves that control movement of the vocal cords, one on each side. If one is injured, the cord on that side becomes flaccid and moves toward the middle. If both are injured, they won't move and may even obstruct the airway requiring a tracheostomy. I assure her that the risk of such injury is only around 1% and that we have a device that allows us to monitor the integrity of the nerve during surgery.

She nods and asks, "Will I be able to sing afterwards?"

I'm ready for this one. The stock response if I say, "Yes" is to say, " Gee that's great because I never could before!"

I give her my stock answer, "Only if you could before."

She gives me a funny look and says, "I'm an operatic voice major at the ASU School of Music."

Nothing like a little pressure.

In addition to the recurrent nerves, I must also worry about the superior laryngeal nerves. These enter the larynx at the top of the thyroid gland and under most circumstances are not considered very important. They cause the vocal cords to tense and flex and are responsible for pitch in the voice. A normal person who loses one or both won't even notice until they try to speak for a long time or shout. Then the voice may be weak and breathy.

An Opera singer uses these nerves to add vibrato to their voice and to sustain notes, especially high notes.

With some trepidation, I take her to surgery and spend a lot of extra time on the dissection and identification of the small nerve trunks. Surgery goes well and her tumor turns out to be a benign adenoma.

A week after surgery she comes in for her postop visit. As she's checking in, my medical assistant, who knows how worried I was about her nerves quietly asks her, "How is your voice?"

She steps back, straightens up, opens her mouth, and hits a high C that she sustains for a full 15 seconds. All the other patients in the waiting room break out in applause.

## Rediscovering First Principles, or Grand Futile Gestures

It was a late night Saturday trauma: a 59-year-old woman in a high speed head on collision. She was not restrained and ended up bend almost double, pinned under the steering wheel and dashboard of her car. Thirty-minute extraction, seventeen minute transport time. We're now three quarters of the way through that first golden hour when rapid intervention can still make a difference.

Her vitals were all over the map in the ambulance, heart rate swinging between the low 60's and up to 120. Her blood pressure would be normal one minute, then drop to the 50's the next.

In the trauma bay we had the low end of that swing. We placed another large bore IV and started pouring in fluids and O negative blood. Her blood pressure briefly rose to the high 90's. She opened her eyes and looked at me. She said, "I can't breathe. Help me." And then she died.

Her blood pressure went away completely, not recordable. Her heart rate, which had been 120, fell to 40 and the pattern changed from normal sinus to a junctional rhythm (the last ditch effort of a dying heart to keep going).

It's called PEA – pulseless electrical activity. The electrical system of the heart is still firing but no contraction is taking place either because the heart is empty or because it can't fill. I bet on the latter and called for the thoracotomy tray.

ER thoracotomy is a dramatic event. It's also usually futile. Survival after opening someone's chest in the ER is less than 10% under most circumstances. A few centers report better results with penetrating trauma.. My personal experience in thirty years is two survivors, one penetrating and one blunt.

I opened her chest through a left lateral incision through the space between the 5th and 6th ribs and extended it across the sternum. Her pericardium, the membrane around her heart, was filled with clot and it was squeezing the heart so it couldn't fill. I opened the pericardium and evacuated the clot and her heart filled and started to beat.

Yes! I thought, watching the ventricle fill and contract. Then I saw the same blood that filled her ventricle rush out of the aortic valve annulus and the darker blood pouring out of the hole in her superior vena cava. She'd avulsed her heart from the superior mediastinum – ripped it off of the major vessels in the upper chest. In about twenty seconds the heart fasciculated and stopped.

First principles - mortality for ER thoracotomy in blunt trauma is 100%. But she opened her eyes and spoke to me. Sometimes you need to make a grand futile gesture, just so you can sleep at night.

A Saturday Trauma Shift

Under 'Better To Be Lucky Than Smart':
An 18 year old male attempting to break the 'car surfing' distance record (I didn't know they kept such records) at mile three was struck in the eye by a bug (no goggles), lost his balance and fell off the car striking his head on the pavement (no helmet either). Despite an occipital skull fracture and a subdural hematoma, he's awake and alert and talking. He's likely to survive to attempt the record again.

Under 'No Cure For Stupid':
A thirty-year-old male, passenger in a car that spun out on the freeway and struck the guardrail. He was unhurt in the crash, but when the police approached he got out of the car, jumped over the guardrail and fell fifteen feet to the bottom of a ravine. He broke his heel and his femur (thighbone) and required a crane to extricate him from the ravine. It seems he had a bag of illegal Oxycontin in his pocket and didn't want the cops to find it. It didn't occur to him to simply toss the bag out the window and retrieve it later. To add insult to injury, the cops say they wouldn't have searched him anyway since he wasn't driving and was unhurt in the original accident.

Under 'No Good Deed Goes Unpunished':
A twenty-year –old male was the designated driver for a buddy's 21st birthday celebration. He did his job, stayed sober and safely delivered all of the partygoers home before heading for home himself. He fell asleep at the wheel and drove the car into a dry canal, shattering his second lumbar vertebra. He has no sensation below mid-thigh and can't bend his legs. Fortunately, the neurosurgeons stabilized his spine and say he has a reasonable chance at a full recovery.

Under 'Only in Arizona':
An amateur cowboy was practicing his roping skills for an upcoming rodeo. He dropped his loop around a practice post, cinched it up tight and went to wrap his end around the pommel of his saddle. For some reason, the horse reared, the rope wound around his thumb as well as the pommel and sheared his thumb off at the

base. The rope then broke, the end whipped back under tension and caught him in the right eye, rupturing the globe (eyeball). He fell from the horse breaking some ribs and the horse stepped on him breaking his femur. Four major injuries from a single freak event.

Every shift is a new adventure.

Making the Cut

I have wanted to be a surgeon for as long as I can remember. Despite that wish, I was incredibly naïve about the process of becoming one. I vaguely knew one had to graduate from college and go to medical school, but even as a high school senior had no clue how one went about getting into med school. There was an accepted premed track at the University of Illinois, but I blithely ignored it. Whether this was out of hubris or willful ignorance, I am still not sure.

My choice of college was constrained by financial considerations. By the time I graduated from high school, I was basically estranged from my family. The reasons for this are many and not terribly relevant anymore, but I was on my own from the age of 18. I had won a state academic scholarship that would pay tuition and fees for any state school in Illinois, and the U of I at Urbana was the only choice I considered.

I was a very good student in high school. I learned early on that academic success carried rewards and could be my ticket out of the chaos of my home life. I scored higher on the Advanced Placement Biology test than any other student in the state, and 99% of those nationwide. I qualified for almost a full year of college credit before I even registered at the university.

My time in college was spent mainly in libraries and study halls. I had friends; I even joined a fraternity, although our house was full of engineers and mathematicians who thought complex, technology based practical jokes were the height of humor. But at my core, I was a 'grind', a student focused on studying to the exclusion of almost anything else. What my education lacked were the usual liberal arts courses – history, philosophy, literature. I had a single introductory philosophy course and two semesters of a foreign language (Norwegian, which I have totally forgotten other than a couple of stock phrases) in order to fulfill basic requirements. Otherwise, it was all science and math; everything on the prerequisite list for most med schools and a lot more physiology and biochemistry than necessary.

I studied obsessively. I took practice tests for fun. In the end, I finished a degree in physiology in just three years. I also scored highly on the Medical College Admissions Test. I thought I had it made.

Little did I realize that every other prospective medical student was working just as hard as I was, and most of them had a PLAN. They were carefully cultivating professional recommendations, research credits, and extracurricular activities to round out an entire 'package' for an admissions committee. All I had was good grades and a high MCAT score. Both were a dime a dozen among medical school applicants.

I applied to six schools, not an excessively long list but more than many and the limit of what I could afford. (Application fees ranged from $150 to over $1000). I was asked to interview at four, which in retrospect should have surprised me. I didn't have the polished CV that many of my peers boasted. I suspect a couple of good recommendations from a physiology professor and a friend's father, himself a surgeon, may have helped. I was full of confidence that my medical career was in the bag.

Then came the rejection letters. First Harvard, which was OK since I didn't really want to go there. Then Stanford followed by Duke, Wake Forest and the Medical College of South Carolina (My girlfriend of the time had moved to Charleston. Not a good way to choose a school but I was in love). That left only the University of Illinois College of Medicine.

In November, I got a thin letter from the U of I admissions office. My heart sank. Thin letters meant rejection. Thick letters contained registration paperwork and meant you'd been accepted.

I didn't open the letter right away. I wandered the Quad for a day, thinking, worrying, and trying to plan my next move. I decided I would remain an undergrad for another year and add biochemistry to my degree, retake the MCAT, and try to cultivate some more professors for recommendation letters.

I went home and opened the letter, expecting the usual 'Thank you for your interest but . . .' Instead, the first word was 'Congratulations'. I was in. Registration information would be sent separately once I confirmed my acceptance of admission. I sent back the little confirmatory post card enclosed with the letter within an hour. I had made the first cut of my career.

A Surgeons Day

It was a quintessential General Surgery day. An elective line up that started with a complex abdominal hernia repair, followed by a thyroid lobectomy, a laparoscopic cholecystectomy (removing a gallbladder with the laparoscope) and finishing with a robotic laparoscopic Nissen fundoplication (fixing a hiatal hernia and wrapping the esophagus to prevent acid reflux). Halfway through the second procedure, an internist friend of mine called me. Bad sign - he never calls personally unless it's a disaster.

"Are you busy?" he asks. Another bad sign. He's not given to small talk and that kind of lead-in means he needs a favor.

"What's up?" I ask. He jumps right in. He has a patient in the ER with abdominal pain and a CT scan showing a perforated colon. Probably diverticulitis, but there's a lot of spillage and free air in the abdomen. Free air means that air from the intestine is leaking into the abdominal cavity and showing up in places where air doesn't belong. The implication of free air is that the leak is large and the body can't wall it off. Peritonitis usually follows. So far, a pretty standard presentation for a perforated diverticulum of the colon, serious but not disastrous.

"What's the rest of the story?" I ask. After an apology for dumping this on me, he fills in the details. The patient has emphysema. She has poor oxygen saturations on a good day and now is hypoxic, blue, hypotensive, and getting emergently intubated as we speak. She is on high dose steroids for her lungs and her rheumatoid arthritis. She has had two strokes and a blood clot in her lung and is on Coumadin, a powerful blood thinner. Her INR, a measure of her prolonged clotting time due to the drug, is 4.5 (normal clotting is 1).

Surgeons hate Coumadin. It's hard to control and not easily reversed in an emergency. We also hate steroids. They inhibit the immune system so patients are more susceptible to infection. They delay wound healing, so patients on high doses are at risk for wound breakdown. This lady is a train wreck. She would not be a candidate for an elective procedure under any circumstances, but this is no longer an elective situation.

I finish the thyroid operation, which fortunately was not a cancer, speak to the family, and then hustle over to the ER. Mrs. G.

is now intubated and has a couple of large bore IV lines in. My internist friend has started antibiotics, gotten some blood typed and crossed (with her coagulation profile, we're going to need it), and started pressors (drugs like epinephrine that raise the blood pressure) because she's now in septic shock. Dr. K. is one of the good ones; an internist who follows his own patients when they are admitted and who is comfortable with seriously ill people. The only thing I add is a dose of recombinant Factor VII.

Factor VII is a clotting factor in the coagulation cascade. It used to be precipitated from donor blood and is used for hemophilia. It's now manufactured by recombinant DNA technology and is free of human pathogens. It's also beastly expensive and dispensed by the microgram. An off-label use is in the severely bleeding patient and as a temporary reversing agent in patients on Coumadin. It buys you a couple of hours before it metabolizes away and the blood stops clotting again. We use it as a bridge in situations like this where anticoagulated patients need an immediate operation. There are other agents that can be used, but they are all either riskier or take a long time to work.

I bump myself (delay my other cases and use my room and anesthesiologist for this case) and we rush off to the OR. The operation is pretty straightforward. I take out the perforated segment of colon, oversew the downstream end as a blind rectal pouch and bring out the upstream end as a colostomy. We close the abdomen with some retention sutures, extra heavy sutures through the big abdominal muscles. Two hours, five units of packed red cells and four units of plasma later, we transfer the patient to the intensive care unit.

I'm now two hours behind schedule and have the hardest part of my day coming up. The laparoscopic cholecystectomy is easy and the patient is a young healthy woman. She does well and will go home from the recovery room.

The robotic case is much different. Robotic surgery is a misnomer. Remote teleoperation surgery is more accurate. The robot does nothing on its own. It is a tool, an extension of my hands. I sit at a console, several feet away from the patient and operate the arms and manipulators of the robot with fingertip controls. My head is in a hood with binocular eyepieces that give me three-dimensional vision through the robot's two cameras. It's just like having my head inside the patient, up close to the area where I'm operating. The drawback is the complete lack of any tactile sensation. Even with the regular laparoscopic instruments, I can still 'feel' what's going on. Not the same as with my fingers but like the feel you get using chopsticks to eat. You can tell the texture of the food, it's size and resistance to tearing. Regular laparoscopic surgery is similar. I can tell if tissue is hard or soft, weak or sturdy by the feedback sensation through the instrument. Not so with the robot. It's all visual.

Robotic cases are stressful. Even after a hundred or so, I still feel stressed while operating. I don't schedule more than one a day and would prefer not to have other hard cases on the same day. This day, I've already been stressed and am not looking forward to the robot. Fortunately, my patient is a healthy man and is reasonably thin. The case starts well and by twenty minutes in, we have the robot docked, the instruments in and I move to the console to start work.

That's when the pages from the ICU start. Mrs. G. is still bleeding, soaking through her dressing and leaking from the edges of her colostomy. Her INR is 3; better than before but still too high. I order more plasma and some vitamin K. Fresh Frozen Plasma (FFP) is full of clotting factors and helps reverse the Coumadin. So does Vitamin K. (Coumadin blocks vitamin K which is necessary in the manufacture of the clotting factors by the liver).

Throughout the robotic operation, I field calls from the ICU. My mind has to be able to split attention between the operation at hand and the resuscitation of my critical patient in the ICU. I also maintain a low level of situational awareness for the room around me - what my assistant nurse is doing, how the monitors of the patients pulse and BP read, whether the anesthesiologist is relaxed or busy - all these things are there in the background.

The robot surgery goes well. We finish in a little under three hours, about par for that type of surgery. I'm convinced it would have gone faster without the interruptions from the ICU, but don't worry much about it. It's a decent time and I feel like I still know what's going on with Mrs. G. I write post op orders and talk to the family before returning to the ICU.

Mrs. G has stabilized somewhat. She's off the pressors and the oozing seems to have slowed down. Her saturations are terrible, but survivable, and probably as good as she ever gets. More importantly, her base deficit (a measure of acid in the blood) is -3, which means she's delivering oxygen to her tissues adequately. The shock seems to be clearing and her INR is down to 1.5. Now we only have her lungs and kidneys to worry about. But at least I can go home. It's nine P.M. and I've been in the hospital since six in the morning.

      It's not that this day was so special. Quite the contrary. Many days are less busy, some more so. The day was not unusual for me or for many of my colleagues, which is why we are becoming dinosaurs. Few choose to go into surgery these days, fewer into General Surgery. That broad range of skills and orientation is slipping away, replaced by specialists who concentrate on single organ systems or disciplines. I don't know if this is a good or bad thing. Specialists can concentrate on the latest knowledge and techniques but sometimes miss the bigger picture. I still think the ability to shift gears rapidly between a routine schedule and an emergency and then back again still has value. I don't see that ability in my successors coming out of today's training programs.

The Shooting Gallery

I started my first surgical clerkship in September of my third year in medical school with high hopes for a good experience. This was what I had come to medical school for. It was all I had ever wanted to do. I wasn't disappointed. I know my perceptions of that rotation were colored by enthusiasm and expectation, but I found that even the mundane aspects of surgery, the things the other students complained about, were fascinating to me.

I enjoyed writing fluid and electrolyte orders. I loved being in the operating room, even standing for an hour holding a liver retractor while the resident took out a gallbladder. I didn't care that I couldn't see the field. The interplay between the surgeons, the instrumentation, the environment, all provided lessons to be absorbed. I read voraciously from the textbook, studied and reviewed anatomy, tied knots on the leg of my desk until my fingers were raw and I was literally tying in my sleep.

When the residents sat around and talked at lunch or after rounds, I hung around the periphery like a puppy, listening.

I even managed to take something away from Dr. Baker's Shooting Gallery (although even I couldn't say I enjoyed it). The Gallery was a Saturday morning ritual. Every Saturday at 9:00 AM all the students on surgical rotations anywhere in the University of Illinois system were required to appear in Dr. Baker's office. He would then fire questions at us. If you answered correctly, he would ask another question, and then another, until you got one wrong or didn't know the answer. Then he'd assign some lengthy reading in that subject area and a written synopsis of what you read, to be turned in by Wednesday. Everyone hated him and his Shooting Gallery.

I didn't enjoy it, but I did learn a lot and it started the process of learning to think on my feet.

About four weeks into the twelve-week clerkship, I was hanging around the operating room desk at five in the evening. I had no duties that night and had found that if I was in the right place at the right time, I could scrub in to cases that I hadn't been posted for. Usually these were emergency procedures or late cases being done by one of the private practice Attendings.

I was looking over the bulletin board where the cases were posted when I became aware of a shadow behind me. I turned to find Dr. Baker regarding me.

"Mr. Davis, isn't it?" he said.

"Yes sir."

"Is your service on duty tonight?"

"No, sir."

"Have you finished your ward duties?"

"Yes, sir. The residents went over to the Greeks for dinner, but the rounds are done."

"Have you finished your reading on the Tetralogy of Fallot?" he asked, recalling my assignment from Saturday's Shooting Gallery.

"Yes, sir. The synopsis is on your desk."

He looked up at the board and rubbed his chin. "Very well. Come with me. I'm taking Dr. Jones through his first incarcerated hernia this evening. You will assist him."

I followed eagerly, if with some trepidation. I had read up on hernias for an earlier case, but had never seen an incarcerated one.

A hernia is nothing more than a defect in the abdominal wall or other structure that allows tissue or organs to enter a space from which they are normally excluded. The common places for hernias in the abdomen are the groins and the umbilicus (belly button). Incarceration is when something gets into the hernia and gets stuck there. It actually isn't all that common with an incidence of only 1 or 2 percent in most hernias. Not much comfort if you're the one it happens to, but not common nevertheless.

Dr. Jones was a second year resident that I knew only by sight, since he was on another surgical service. He was less than enthusiastic about having me as an assistant, but Dr. Baker made it clear that he would scrub the case as well.

As we stood at the scrub sink working the soap and stiff brushes over our hands, Dr. Baker grilled Jones on the steps of the operation. I was relieved to have been spared any questions.

I had watched hernia surgery a couple of times, but had never assisted on one. Dr. Baker stood next to Jones and directed me to the opposite side of the table, the first assistant's position. We marked off the field with towels and draped the patient.

As soon as Dr. Jones made his first incision, Dr. Baker began questioning me on the anatomy of the inguinal canal and all the structures in the groin. This was stuff I knew cold from the anatomy lab, but in living tissue, it looked different. I managed to correctly identify things with a little subtle help from Dr. Jones. He'd surreptitiously point to structures Dr. Baker was asking me about.

After a few minutes it started to make more sense and I found myself getting into the flow of the surgery. It was my first experience with the Dance. Assisting in an operation is like dancing with a partner. He leads; you follow and try to make him look smooth. I found myself anticipating Jones and moving retractors around to show him what he needed to see. Even Dr. Baker stopped asking questions as we got the incarcerated bowel exposed and reduced into the abdomen.

I don't remember if Dr. Baker resumed his questions. I must have done all right with them, though, because he didn't assign me any reading during the operation.

Dr. Baker left the room as Jones and I were tying the last skin stitches.

"Thanks," Dr. Jones said, shaking my hand. "You were better help than I expected. Tell Carmody I said you were OK." Dr. Carmody was the Attending on my service. I didn't think he'd appreciate me giving him a message from a junior resident, but I thanked him anyway.

Dr. Baker had left a note pinned to the bulletin board.

"Mr. Davis, read chapters 20 and 21 in Dr. Nyhus' book HERNIA and report on your reading by Saturday's question period. You were an adequate assistant but need to review the Bassini and McVay repairs."

I sighed and headed to the medical library.

Ruptures and Redo's

Today was hernia day in the office. That wasn't the intent; it was just the way the referrals came in. Four out of five new patients this afternoon had either complex or recurrent hernias. I seem to have acquired a reputation as the go-to guy for difficult hernias. It wasn't something I sought out. In fact, it's something I wouldn't mind losing. I don't know if I get these cases because I get good results, or if it's just a matter of, "Hey, let's call Davis. He'll operate on anything."

Hernia surgery is one of the most under rated aspects of general surgery. A hernia repair is likely the first real operation you do in training, usually as an intern. Both the patient and the surgeon regard hernia repairs as relatively minor procedures. After more years than I care to think about in this business, I have come to appreciate the herniorhaphy as an operation that is simple and elegant in its conception and sometimes devilishly difficult in its execution.

A hernia is nothing more than a gap or hole in the abdominal wall through which stuff from the inside can poke through creating the characteristic bulge. The abdominal wall, beneath the skin, is a sandwich of muscle and fascia. (Fascia is the tough white connective tissue that binds muscles together – think of the gristle in a cheap steak). There are natural gaps between muscle groups and normal openings in the wall that allow structures to pass through. Spontaneous hernias tend to occur through these areas. The most common locations for spontaneous hernias are the groin and the umbilicus (belly button).

Adult spontaneous hernias should be repaired with some kind of reinforcing mesh or tissue. Direct repair with suture alone has a fifteen to thirty percent risk of recurrence. A huge VA study in the late 1980's proved the superiority and safety of mesh repairs and it has been the standard of care ever since.

Incisional hernias are more complex. As the name implies, these occur through old incisions either due to infection or just poor wound healing. Under the best of circumstances, a midline abdominal incision has a ten percent chance of giving rise to a hernia, often many years later. Any first repair has about the same ten percent risk of recurrence. Any subsequent repair adds another ten percent risk, that is, twenty percent for a second repair, thirty percent for a third repair and so on. The risk of recurrence tops out at about fifty percent, but at that point the statistics have little to do with individual patients. Fixing these hernias can be particularly challenging. Fixing them after a couple of recurrences can be downright intimidating.

One of my new patients has had ten prior abdominal operations, and three prior ventral hernia repairs, none by me. She's as healthy as a morbidly obese 60 year old can be – no known heart disease, no diabetes (surprising) and no pulmonary disease. But her weight alone makes her risk of recurrence high. Several surgeons have already refused to operate on her. (See the first paragraph of this post. Yes, I'm a sucker) There is no realistic expectation that she will lose substantial weight, so requiring that before fixing her hernia is unrealistic. So we will proceed with surgery sometime in the next few weeks.

She will need what is called a component separation. We split the abdominal wall into its component muscle groups. We repair the hernia defect with some kind of mesh or artificial tissue and them move the separated components toward the midline to close the abdominal wall. The exact procedure will depend on the strength and integrity of what muscle remains in her abdominal wall.

I was realistic her. Her overall risk for another recurrence, no matter what how good a job I do is forty to fifty percent. I have no clear idea what I will actually do once we get into the operating room. This is a situation where I literally make it up as I go along. I may be able to find enough sturdy tissue to do a repair. I may need to reconstruct part or all of her abdominal wall with a human tissue graft – cadaver skin that has been processed into a leathery patch we can use to repair defects where the bowel or viscera will be exposed to the patch. Synthetic mesh and bowel are a bad combination leading to scarring, erosion, perforation and infection. Every surgery like this is a new adventure. And as Zane Grey said, "Adventure is just another word for trouble that smart people learn to avoid."

The Purse Thief

It was the final two weeks of my third year surgical clerkship and my service was covering trauma. In 1976 the concept of a dedicated trauma center was still in its infancy. Studies were being published at that time demonstrating better outcomes in hospitals that did a higher volume of acute trauma and the concept of the 'Golden Hour', that first hour after a major injury when interventions were most effective at saving lives, was being promoted. But an organized approach to trauma was only being done in a few places.

At Cook County Hospital, where I was doing my clerkship, the trauma service was covered by one of the general surgery services on a weekly basis. It had been quiet the first two days of the week with only a couple of admissions and no surgeries. The Chief Resident, Dr. Kolpitz, and I were trolling the ER, checking out the incoming patients for potential new admissions.

In the first ER cubicle was a very obese woman complaining loudly about arm pain. Her left arm was in a sling and the student nurse was struggling to help her out of her dress. The woman wasn't making it easy, demanding that the nurse be careful and not stretch the seams of her dress as she tried to work it off of her injured arm.

Kolpitz checked the chart on the door and then returned it.

"Humerus fracture, ground level fall. Nothing for us," he said.

The woman saw him. "Are you a Doctor?" she demanded.

"Yes, ma'am," he said. "I'm a surgeon."

"Well I want to know when someone is going to look at my arm. I can't wait here all day. I've got to go to the police station and report a robbery."

"I'm sure the orthopedic surgeon will be here shortly," said Kolpitz. "I'll have the charge nurse contact the police. They have representatives here. Maybe they can take the report from you."

He walked away as the woman began ranting again. I trailed after him.

A few minutes later, as we completed our circuit of the ER, an ambulance pulled up to the intake doors. We watched as the paramedics unloaded what looked like a section of wooden fence. Only as they turned toward the trauma bays did we see the thin man lying on his side with his back to the wooden planks. Protruding from his abdomen, just below the breastbone was a sword. A more careful look showed that the tip of the sword was embedded in the wooden plank at his back.

The rule with impalement injuries is to leave the impaling object in place until it can be removed in the operating room. The object may be plugging a hole in a major blood vessel and once it is removed, the vessel can be free to bleed massively. The patient is brought in with the object in place.

Rather than try to dislodge the tip of the sword from the wood and risk torqueing the blade or inadvertently dislodging something, the medics had brought the section of fencing to which the man was pinned.

"Now this is interesting," said Kolpitz as he followed the medics toward trauma 4.

Just as they passed the obese woman in cubicle one, she let out a shriek and charged toward the man.

"That's the S.O.B. who stole my purse. I'll kill him. I'll kill that damn thief."

The poor student nurse tried to hold her back but was brushed aside like an annoying fly. Kolpitz stepped forward but the security guard beat him to it. The woman screamed as the guard jostled her fracture, but it slowed her enough for the medics to get by and reach the trauma bay. More security guards showed up then and the woman was convinced to return to her own cubicle. She went, complaining loudly and demanding to see a police officer. We hurried after the impaled man.

The sword was a thin rapier, about two feet long and buried almost to the hilt in the man's abdomen. The tip was driven about an inch into the rough wood of the fence. The hilt was only a few inches from his breastbone. It was finely made, real ivory inlaid with some kind of black wood. All in all, an elegant looking weapon.

Kolpitz secured the blade as it exited the patient's back with a large clamp and the paramedics and I worked the plank off of the tip. There was very little bleeding.

The patient was conscious and alert. "That bitch tried to kill me," he said. "She stabbed me with a sword over a cheap ass purse with only seven dollars in it." Lovely fellow.

Bit by bit the story came out. He was a junkie looking for cash for his next fix. He spotted the obese lady with her purse draped over her shoulder and an umbrella in her hand. He tried to snatch the purse on the run, but the lady wasn't going to let go. She pulled back and they both fell. He ended up with the purse and she broke her arm. He managed to get up and ran around the corner. He never expected her to follow him. Just as he took the money and tossed the purse away, she barreled down on him. She pushed him up against the fence, whipped the blade out of the shaft of her umbrella, and ran him through with all of her considerable bulk behind it.

We took him to the operating room and removed the blade. Luckily for him, it had missed the major blood vessels. He had a through and through hole in his stomach and some muscle damage in his back, but that was about all.

Sadly, the cops arrested the fat lady. Concealed blades more than three inches long are illegal in Chicago, and while they agreed that her attack on him was justified, maybe even self-defense, the type of weapon left them no choice. The ER staff took up a collection to pay her bail.

Regulations

In early 1981 I was a second year resident at Bethesda Naval Hospital on the general surgery service when a very high-ranking Admiral was admitted with an acute abdomen. He was a major VIP, way up in the Pentagon command structure. As a lowly resident, I had little to do with his care. The Chief of Surgery did his operation and rounds were made by attending surgeons only – no students, interns or residents. The Chief Residents were introduced to this august person but had no hand in his care.

This was the norm for bigwigs. We had Congressmen and Senators, Cabinet Secretaries, even the President, admitted to the hospital at various times during my training. These were the only times when protocol overrode surgical education.

The thing was, even though we peons were excluded, the day-to-day care of these VIP's fell to the regular ward nurses and corpsmen. There were special hospital rooms on each ward for these special patients, but the regular ward staff covered them.

The Admiral was admitted to the surgical floor after a routine procedure for an anticipated three- or four-day stay if everything went well. He wasn't an unreasonable patient, but he was accustomed to command. The role of patient didn't suit him. He spent a lot of time on the phone communicating with his staff, and often disregarded or put off attempts by the nurses and corpsmen to do routine postop care.

After the second day, he began to run a low-grade fever. The attending rounding that day spoke to the nurse and left orders that the Admiral get up and walk and do some deep breathing exercises. Early postop fevers are often due to small airway collapse in the lungs called atelectasis. If the patient takes deep breaths and reopens those airways, the fever resolves. If he doesn't, more airways collapse as pressure equalizes across the alveoli and eventually it can lead to pneumonia.

The junior nurse was intimidated by the Admiral's rank, and when he refused her request to get out of bed and walk and breath, saying he was too tired, she fled the room and went to the charge nurse.

The charge nurse that day was Lieutenant Freda. She was a trusted colleague of mine at the time. (We later became much closer, so much so that I married her). She had only been in the Navy for a year, her rank coming from her advanced nursing degree and work experience.

She went to the Admiral's room and found him sitting in his bed, reading documents.

"Good afternoon, Admiral," she said. "I'm Lieutenant Freda. I'm the charge nurse on the ward today. How are you feeling?"

"I'm fine, Lieutenant," he said dismissively. "Just tired and I have a lot of work to do."

"Of course, sir," Lieutenant Freda said. "May I ask you a question about the chain of command?"

"What about it?"

"Well, if I remember the Bluejacket Manual correctly, the Officer of the Deck on a ship's bridge has command, even if there is a senior officer present. The senior officer must follow the orders of the OOD unless he formally relieves him and takes command himself. Is that correct, sir?"

"Yes, Lieutenant. That's correct." The Admiral smiled. "Most nurses didn't pay that much attention to the Manual during OCS. Why do you ask?"

"Because, sir, this is my bridge, and as charge nurse, I am the OOD." She smiled. "Unless you intend to relieve me. Do you?"

"No, Lieutenant."

"Then these are the orders of the day. You will get out of bed and walk three times around the nurse's station. Then, you will do the deep breathing exercises that Dr. C. has ordered. After that you can return to your papers, but I will return in four hours and we will do the walk again. You are at risk for blood clots in your legs and pneumonia if you just sit in bed all day and don't get up."

The Admiral frowned and started to fume, then stopped himself and laughed. "All right, Lieutenant. Whatever you say."

He got out of bed and Lieutenant Freda helped him walk for the first forty feet, then he went on without help.

One of the corpsmen related the story to me later and I confirmed it with her on evening rounds.

"It was disrupting the routine on the ward and I couldn't let him intimidate my corpsmen that way," she said.

I think I started to fall in love with her right then. I'd never met a nurse who could quote the Bluejacket Manual to the Chief of

Naval Operations and get away with it. I found her incredibly exciting then, and still do to this day.

Herman

In 1979 I was the battalion medical officer for NMCB-5, a Naval Construction Battalion deployed to Diego Garcia in the Indian Ocean. We were part of a big buildup going on at that time and the battalion was working on several major projects – new barracks, a runway extension, utilities upgrades and a new fuel pier. We had a group of divers attached to us who were responsible for welding and inspection on the large caissons that would form the footings under the pier.

This was dangerous work. The water was clear and warm but the atoll was deep and the divers were working at 60 to 90 feet for the upper limits of their safe bottom time. To add to the risk, there was no decompression chamber on the island. The closest chamber was at Subic Bay in the Philippines, a 12-hour flight away.

Diego Garcia is a coral atoll that is about as far from anything as on can get in the Indian Ocean. Its isolation has made it a sea life and wildlife paradise. The reefs are pristine and the fish and corals would make it a prime dive destination if it weren't a military base.

One resident of the lagoon was well known to the construction crew on the pier project. Herman was the name they had given to a huge hammerhead shark that regularly swam in the area. We thought he was male, but my marine biologist son tells me that the female hammerheads are usually larger, so maybe Hermione would have been a better name. Male or female, it was a big shark - well over twenty feet long. We knew this because he had been observed on the surface next to the gig, a utility boat that was 20 feet in length and Herman was longer than the boat.

One afternoon one of the divers was down at about 60 feet checking welds on the latest caisson installation. He finished his inspection and turned to start his ascent when he found himself face to face with Herman. It's not clear whether Herman really intended to have the diver for a midafternoon snack or if the diver just freaked out at the sight of jaws big enough to swallow a medium sized cow.

The diver shot to the surface without the usual slow ascent and decompression stops. He managed to climb out of the water before his legs stopped working and he doubled up with joint pain.

The bends, or more accurately decompression sickness, occurs when dissolved gasses, mostly nitrogen, suddenly come out of solution and form bubbles in tissues and blood vessels. At depth, gas dissolves in higher concentration that at sea level. When a diver ascends from depth, he must do it slowly so that the dissolved gas returns to the lungs and can be respired. Decompression stops at various depths for several minutes are often included in the dive profile to allow for this gas clearance. Coming up suddenly in an uncontrolled ascent can lead to serious damage as the bubbles form in tissue and blood vessels. The joints are the most common areas affected, followed by the spinal cord, brain and arteries.

Treatment of the bends involves using a decompression chamber, a chamber or room that can be pressurized to the equivalent of several atmospheres of pressure. The patient is returned to depth, or at least the same pressure as the depth of his dive and then is brought up slowly to allow the gas to be cleared. The process is called 'diving' the patient. Often it takes several dives in the chamber to remove all of the bubbles and sometimes there is permanent damage done before the gas can be cleared. The faster the patient gets to the chamber after the onset of symptoms, the better the prognosis.

Our diver was clearly 'bent' and possibly had an arterial gas embolus (bubble) in a spinal artery. We needed to get him to Subic Bay and the decompression chamber as fast as possible. Without a chamber there wasn't much we could do other than pain medication and high concentrations of oxygen. (Elevating the oxygen tension in the blood may pull some of the nitrogen bubbles back into solution).

We called to airfield but the only aircraft on the ground was the C-141 that had arrived that morning on the weekly supply and personnel run and it was getting ready to return to Clark Air Base. We called the tower, held the outbound flight, and loaded the diver onto the ambulance. We got clearance from the Air Force to commandeer their plane and got the patient onboard.

The other doctor on the island, an internist by training, and I did rock, paper, scissors to see who would go with the diver. I won (or lost, depending on your point of view) and climbed aboard as well. I told the pilots we had to keep the plane pressured at sea level. Any further decrease in air pressure at altitude would release more gas and increase the size of the bubbles already in the tissue.

The pilot grinned and said, "No problem, Doc."

We took off and instead of the sharp climb that I expected, we rose slowly into the air and then held altitude at about 500 feet. The plane leveled off and there we stayed; 500 feet off the water, all the way to the Philippines. I was allowed to come up into the cockpit as we roared down the Strait of Malacca, one of the busiest shipping channels in the world. Deck crews and fishermen ducked and scrambled for cover as we passed over. Maybe they thought the big lumbering cargo plane was a bomber, or that it was going to crash.

We made it to Clark and offloaded the diver for the short flight on a navy patrol plane to Subic Bay. They dove him within an hour of arrival there, about 14 hours into his decompression sickness. He stayed at Subic for six more dives over eight days and made a complete recovery.

I later found out that the pilot's stunt was not necessary; he could have kept the plane pressurized to sea level at any altitude. But I'm sure he had a lot of fun buzzing the Strait of Malacca at close to 500 mph. I stayed in the BOQ at Clark for a day and caught the next 141 back to Diego. With me on that flight was Ensign Bossa carrying a mysterious aluminum briefcase, but that's another story.

The Etiquette of Help

"Any surgeon to OR 6 STAT. Any surgeon to OR 6 STAT."

No surgeon wants to hear or respond to a call like that. It means someone is in deep *kim chee* and needs help right away.

I was in the locker room, just about to strip off my scrubs and dress to go out with my wife for the evening. We had finished a full day of routine surgery – two gallbladders and a colon resection – and had plans for dinner. Our older son was home from college and had offered to watch his younger brother for us.

I closed my locker and walked back out to the OR control desk. Michele, my wife and first assistant, was already there. A glance at the control board showed me that Dr. S. was in room 6. She was a gynecologist and according to the board was doing a routine diagnostic laparoscopy. The bustle of technicians and nurses running in and out of the room indicated that it was anything but routine.

We made our way to the room and I stuck my head in. My friend Jon was the anesthesiologist. He was squeezing a bag of packed red blood cells to make them run into the IV faster.

"We could use some help," he said, calmly as ever. But he rolled his eyes toward the table.

Dr. S. stood there, blood coating her arms and chest, her eyes looking at me but somehow also looking far away, the thousand yard stare of someone out of their depth and very afraid.

"Hey, Lou," I said, using her first name as I stepped into the room. Michele followed me and began speaking quietly to the circulating nurse.

"What's going on?" I asked as I looked over her shoulder. The patient's abdomen was open and Lou had her hand deep inside. The abdomen was full of blood, but it didn't seem to be increasing in volume. Whatever was bleeding, Lou seemed to have controlled it by putting her hand in.

"I think I hit a big vessel with my initial trocar," she said, referring to the hollow tube that was used to introduce a laparoscope into the abdomen.

The initial insertion is always blind and there's a risk that the sharp tip of the introducer may hit bowel or blood vessels. The first thing a surgeon does on looking in with the scope is to make sure there hasn't been an inadvertent injury. Lou had seen blood rapidly filling the abdomen and had made a bigger incision right away.

"Is it mesenteric or retroperitoneal," I asked, keeping my voice calm and matter of fact.

"I can't tell. The belly is full of blood. I'm pushing down on the hole I made but don't know what's bleeding."

I had an idea of what she had injured and it made my heart rate bump up a tic. I didn't say anything and forced some calm into my voice as I turned to the circulator. "We'll need the vascular instruments, a Buchwalter retractor and some vascular suture, 3-0 and 4-0."

The circulating nurse was already heading for the door. Michele nodded to me. "Already ordered. I asked them to pull a bowel tray, too. Just in case."

I love my wife for a lot of reasons. Her coolness in a crisis is just one of them. She went to start scrubbing. I turned to Jon.

"Massive transfusion protocol?"

"Already called," he said. "First cooler in five minutes."

"I'm going to scrub," I told Lou. "Just hold pressure and let Jon catch up." She nodded, visibly calmer.

There's an art to coming in to help a colleague in trouble. Most of us have been in that situation, both giving and receiving help. A scheduled case that goes bad is different from a trauma. In trauma, you expect the worst. Your thinking and expectations are already looking for trouble. In a routine case, trouble is an unwelcome surprise and even an experienced surgeon may have difficulty shifting from routine to crisis mode.

The first thing to remember when stepping into a bad situation is that you are the cavalry. You didn't create the situation and recriminations and blame have no place in the room. You need to be the calm center to a storm that started before you got involved. Sometimes that's all that is needed. A fresh perspective, a few focused questions and the operating surgeon can calm down and get back on track.

Other times you need to intervene directly. This is harder to do in a way that doesn't seem confrontational or condescending. The operating surgeon may be out of his or her depth, but this is still their patient. You are the consultant. You need to offer your service with respect, but not shrink from taking action if the patient is truly at risk. Lou had asked for help and was clearly relieved that we were there.

We finished the scrub and gowned up. The monitors showed that the blood and Lou's holding pressure had helped. The patient's pulse was slower and the blood pressure, though still low, was stable.

I extended Lou's incision as she continued to hold pressure. Michele, meanwhile set up the Buchwalter, a self-retaining retractor that freed up the assistant's hands by keeping the abdominal wall open. I could see where the bleeding was coming from, much slower but still welling up from the retroperitoneum – the area behind the intestine near the backbone.

With Michele helping to retract, I opened the space above Lou's hand and got my fingers around the aorta. I told Lou to release her pressure. Blood gushed up until I pushed down on the aorta. The bleeding slowed to a steady ooze. Lou retracted the root of the bowel aside and exposed the hole her trocar had made. It had punctured the anterior wall of the aorta. The hole was still bleeding slowly from blood back filling the vessel from collaterals. Now that I could see it, I put my finger directly in the hole and released the pressure from above. We now had control of the active bleeding. With Michele and Lou's help, I dissected out the aorta above and below the hole and got vascular clamps on. The hole was about a centimeter in diameter, clean edged and easy to repair. We let some blood back bleed to flush out any clots, and then fixed it with some of the vascular suture.

Once we were done and the patient stable, I asked Lou, "Do you want me to stay and help close?"

The acute crisis was over, the patient was stable and I was offering Lou a chance to take back control of the operation. It was more than just letting her save face. It reestablished the doctor-patient relationship she had begun when she first saw the patient. It confirmed for her and the rest of the room that this was still her patient, her case.

"No, I'm OK. Will you write orders for the ICU?"

"Of course."

Michele volunteered to stay and help close the abdomen and I went to take care of the orders.

The patient recovered after a brief stay in the ICU and went home in less than a week.

The point of the story is that at some time, everyone gets in over his or her head. It has happened to me and will again some day. The primary role of the surgeon called upon for help is to not inflame the situation more. Everyone in that operating room is already having a very bad day. Your job, if you respond to such a call, is to get the operation back on track so the patient can be stabilized and the damage repaired. Then you need to back off and acknowledge that the primary responsibility has been returned to the original team.

We never did make it to dinner. My wife often jokes, "You take me to the nicest places." but she knows how much I appreciate her when the crap hits the fan.

Handling Risk

"For sheer unadulterated ego, no one is a match for fighter pilots. Except maybe surgeons. Surgeons are in a class by themselves." Tom Wolfe, *The Right Stuff*

The popular perception of surgeons is similar to the popular perception of fighter pilots. Arrogant self-confidence, disdain for thoughtful planning and reflection, quick to take action - 'shoot first, ask questions later', reckless courage in the face of danger, all are considered typical of the personality type.

Like all stereotypes, there is an element of truth behind the perception. Both surgeons and fighter pilots do jobs that are inherently unnatural. There is nothing 'natural' about flying a machine at speeds faster than the sound made by its own engines. There is nothing 'natural' about cutting into another human being's body and rearranging its anatomy.

Performing at a high level in these arenas requires a special kind of confidence in one's own ability and judgment, a confidence that is often mistaken for arrogance. The willingness to take action in the face of uncertainty, to make irrevocable decisions based on incomplete information, is often mistaken for recklessness. Acceptance of personal responsibility for the consequences of those actions may be mistaken for a disdain for cooperative effort.

I know several former fighter pilots. They'd all make good surgeons. And contrary to the popular perception, they are some of the most conservative and risk averse people I know. I don't mean politically conservative, although most surgeons and pilots tend to identify with that end of the political spectrum. I mean conservative in the sense of resistance to change, reliance on personal responsibility over group responsibility, and acceptance of adverse consequences when a decision goes sideways.

Those who are forced to deal with risk on a daily basis develop ways to both mitigate and tolerate it. Doing the same thing, the same way, every time is one strategy. Checklists and pre-flight or preoperative planning are others. Some of these behaviors and strategies are based on controlled studies of the best, least risky ways to accomplish the task. Others are heuristic – we are trained to do it the way our mentors and teachers did and we continue that way because it works. This creates an extreme aversion to change. Change is bad. Change is an invitation to disaster. The only thing worse is change you don't control.

This aversion to risk carries over into life outside the operating room or cockpit. Even when engaged in what some might consider 'risky' sports or recreation, that risk tends to be personal in nature and controlled.

Surgeons are intimately acquainted with risk and its consequences. The ability to tolerate risk and to mitigate it to the extent possible is the mark of a good surgeon. Most of us do this automatically. The calculus of risk versus benefit when assessing a patient is ongoing and often is only a minimally conscious process. Most surgeons are not routinely involved with high-risk patients or procedures. Many consciously avoid them. Trauma and emergency surgery does not offer that opportunity. You take what you get and do your best in the immediate situation.

It Never Gets Easier

You'd think the mowing the grass in your own front yard would be a relatively risk free afternoon activity. Sure you need to be a little careful with a blade spinning at 3500 RPM, but modern dead man clutches make accidental injury unlikely. Sometimes, even the mundane can turn deadly. Last Saturday I was on Trauma call and a page came through for an incoming trauma code, car vs pedestrian incident, intubated in the field, unresponsive. I was expecting the usual combination of head and extremity injuries that we often see when people are hit by moving cars. Instead, my patient was a 60-year-old man with no obvious external signs of trauma, unconscious and intubated with no responses to any stimulation. His pupils were 5mm, not dilated but not normal and fixed, meaning they didn't contract in response to a bright light. This is a bad sign, usually indicative of severe brain injury, bordering on brain death, unless the patient has gotten paralytic drugs, say for a surgery or intubation.

"Did he get drugs in the field?" I asked hopefully.

"No, doc. He took the tube without bucking or gagging, no drugs needed." Again a bad sign.

Then we got the whole story. He had been mowing his front yard, near the sidewalk, when two cars got involved in a minor fender bender in front of his house. As one of them tried to avoid the accident, it went up on the sidewalk and as the other car hit it, its rear fender brushed against my patient. It was a low speed impact. The car was almost stopped when it clipped him. But speed is less important than force in this case and since force is dependent on mass, the barely moving car knocked the man down. Had he fallen to the grass, he would have had nothing more than a bruise on his thigh. Instead, his head struck the engine housing of the mower. The engine cut off as soon as his hands left the dead man clutch, but the engine is made of tempered steel and aluminum, both much harder than the human skull.

We hurried him off to CT where the scan confirmed a basilar skull fracture with a massive intracranial hemorrhage. His brain was already starting to herniate. That means that the pressure of the bleeding in his skull was pushing the base of his brain into the opening that allows the spinal cord to exit. Herniation = death. The neurosurgeons rushed him off to surgery to take the top of his skull off and give the brain room to expand upward instead of down.

    He's still not responding and may be brain dead. Now I have to talk to the family about organ donation and eventual withdrawal of care if the flow studies show his brain is indeed dead. They're obviously in shock. His son keeps saying, "He was only cutting the grass".

    This job never gets easier.

Handling Sin

There's an old adage in Surgery that says: "It takes two years to teach a resident how to operate and another three to teach a resident when not to operate."

Surgery is an active profession. Above all the Surgeon is expected to take action, even when that involves the decision to NOT do surgery.

Surgical sins are different from Medical sins. There are sins of commission – hubris, arrogance, pride, vanity – all of which we are guilty of at one time or another during our careers. Some of them are also surgical strengths depending on the situation.

There are also the sins of omission – carelessness, sloth, ignorance, and perhaps the most egregious, indecision. As a mentor once said, "A surgeon doesn't have to be right, but he has to be certain."

It's incumbent on us by the nature of what we do to people in surgery to be affirmative in making decisions. By that I mean, any decision should be made actively, through consideration of the action we are taking and its potential consequences.

But wait, aren't all decisions made that way? No, not always. Delay, procrastination 'watchful waiting' often lead to a decision of indecision where the patient's condition changes in spite of our attention rather than because of it. If I, as a surgeon, chose not to operate on a patient, it should be because I have a valid reason for expecting that the situation will resolve without surgery, or perhaps because the patient's condition is such that surgery presents an unacceptable risk.

I recently decided not to operate on an elderly woman with free air in her abdomen. Free air means there is air outside of the bowel or lungs where it belongs. It implies a perforation in the bowel or stomach that is leaking stool or intestinal contents. Under most circumstances, it's a surgical emergency.

I looked at this frail woman who was pleasantly demented with a history of heart disease and a recent stroke and thought, *No way*. It was a gut reaction born of a reluctance to take on a complicated and high-risk surgery. I rationalized it by observing that she was having little pain; that the air seemed scattered and was minimal in volume; that the CT that showed the air gave no indication of where the perforation might be and that she had a high risk of complications. I made a good case for NOT doing surgery, but knew it was a rationalization.

At first it seemed like the right decision. I started high dose antibiotics, put her on a limited diet and repeated her labs and x-rays. Her blood tests improved, she had no fever, her pain almost completely resolved and her intestine seemed to be working.

By the fourth day, however, it should have been clear to me that she wasn't getting better. Still, I rationalized and procrastinated. She wasn't getting worse, after all. I couldn't (or more accurately wouldn't) make a decision to abandon my original plan and take her to surgery.

By the seventh day it was obvious even to the internist that not operating wasn't working. I took her to surgery and drained a large intrabdominal abscess and searched throughout her abdomen for the site of the perforation. I never found it. I suspect it was a pinhole perforation in a colon diverticulum, but even with aggressive manipulation of the area, I couldn't demonstrate a hole.

She did not do well after surgery. She got more septic, her lungs and heart started to fail and after a long discussion with the intensive care internist, and me the family decided on palliative care only. She died a few hours later.

I don't know if she would have survived if I had operated sooner. Perhaps the outcome would have been the same. I will never know. But I do know that my decision to not operate, while justifiable on paper, was not motivated by an objective look at her condition. And when it should have been clear that my initial management was failing, I procrastinated. The sin of indecision led to a delay far beyond what was objectively justified.

Anyone who has been in this business for a while can list his or her own secret tally of sins. I have committed sins of hubris, of arrogance, where I over estimated my capabilities and patients suffered and died for it. I have let pride push me to cling to a course of action when I should have changed course, and patients have been harmed. I have allowed fear or indecision or fatigue or stubbornness to hold me back from doing necessary surgery and patients have died. We all remember those cases but we tend to forget the times when we did the right thing. I can name far more patients that I have lost than ones that I have saved.

How a surgeon handles sin is a deeply personal process. I know some surgeons who simply ignore it. They are able to rationalize their actions and put it all down to patient disease, or at worst, a learning experience. Others become paralyzed by the fear of making an error and refuse to get involved in difficult or complex procedures. Still others internalize the guilt, refuse to let it stop them from continuing to take on the challenging or emergent cases, but ultimately pay a price in the form of sleepless nights and endless private second guessing of each decision.

Sometimes we have the opportunity to confess through the Morbidity and Mortality Conference (see M&M, another essay) and receive closure in the form of peer review of our actions. Even when the review recognizes our failing and chastises us for it, the philosophy of 'forgive and remember' is strong and the ritual lends a form of absolution.

Just as often, though, the sin is private. We know in our hearts what really motivated our action, and even when that action appears appropriate to an outside observer, we alone know how we failed. We must handle that and find a way to live with it if we are to serve our patients and retain our sense of purpose.

M and M (not the candy)

Tomorrow I am going to present a case at the Morbidity and Mortality conference. M&M is a time-honored surgical tradition that, ideally, is an open forum for surgeons to give and accept criticism, dissect their errors and try to understand why adverse events happened. Surgery is not an exact craft. It's not like working on an engine or a malfunctioning computer. Every case is different and presents different opportunities to excel or to trip over your own feet.

The exact cases that I'll have to discuss aren't important. Suffice it to say, there was room for improvement in my management. That's okay. As my friend, the late Troy Brinkerhoff used to say, 'Every day's a school day'. We learn by doing, and sometimes by screwing up.

M&M is part of a larger process of peer review. I know the ability of physicians to police themselves has been seriously questioned of late, but in the setting of a peer review meeting, or M&M conference, surgeons tend to be their own harshest critics.

The process of reviewing and discussing another surgeon's complications can be gut wrenching. We all share a common set of experiences from our training, and after a few years in practice, a common case log of operations performed and problems managed. A few key words about a patient's history or the appearance of an x-ray convey a host of potential difficulties and complications that it would take several minutes to describe to the non-surgeon.

Sometimes that shared experience leads to sage nods of understanding when a difficult case is presented. Yes, we understand. We've been there and but for the grace of God it could be one of us dealing with this complication (And thank God it's you and not me). Other times it leads to forehead smacking what-the-hell-were-you-thinking condemnations.

The key to good peer review is an atmosphere of mutual respect and a commitment to confidentiality. Case discussions under the umbrella of peer review are protected from discovery. Nothing we say to or about one another can find its way into a malpractice suit. That may seem a bit cold at first blush. We are talking about patients who have been harmed by a complication of our surgeries. But if we are to be honest and fearless in our examination of these problems, we can't be looking over our shoulders for a subpoena if we admit to an error in judgment or a lapse in attention.

Does it always work that way? Of course not. Honest criticism sometimes degenerates into acrimony. Competing groups use the peer review process to bludgeon one another. But by and large, the system functions. Relations are patched up and the job of a department chairman is to protect the integrity of the M&M conference. Especially when its his own dirty laundry that's about to be aired.

Covering Up

It was early 1983, I was a fourth year resident, and I was in trouble. My program director, Dr. Fletcher, had called me to his office at three in the afternoon, an hour before preop conference, to talk to me about 'recent events on the Gold surgery service'. My service. I knew what he wanted to talk to me about and as I waited outside his office, visions of my surgical career swirling down the toilet filled my head.

Two days earlier I had lied to him about a patient. I had been covering for my Chief Resident. It wasn't the first time.

The general surgery department at Bethesda was divided into three services: Blue and Gold for general surgery and Red for vascular surgery. Each service had three residents (Chief, Fourth Year and Second Year), two interns and various medical students assigned to it. Each of the three Chief Residents ran one of the services on a four-month rotation.

Dr. P. had been my Chief on Gold for three months. I figured I had only one month to go before I rotated to Red and would be done with P forever. These had been the worst three months of my life, worse even than my internship.

I found out early in the first week on Gold that P was a very smart guy who was totally unable care about other people. He was abrupt, demeaning, self-centered and perfectly willing to blame subordinates for his own errors.

Unfortunately, as I said, he was a very smart guy. He talked a great game and covered his ass well. He was extremely well read; he was up to date on the latest research and read extensively about any problem we encountered on the ward. Which was also part of the problem. He passed off rounding duties to me so he could read and research the disease processes we encountered. He sounded great when he presented cases in preop conference, but if asked about a patient's current status, he had no clue.

More than once, I had stepped in and taken responsibility for errors in order to protect my junior resident from P's finger pointing. It had cost me. Residents are graded on their performance quarterly and I knew my next evaluation would not be as good as the previous ones. My in-service exam scores had suffered because I was shouldering much of his work as well as my own and had little time to study.

Why did I do it? In part because I had been thoroughly indoctrinated in my first three years as a resident that patient care always came first. If P didn't do the job, someone had to. That fell to me as the next senior resident. In part because I still believed that you kept faith with your team, both those above and below you.

The current trouble began three days earlier. We had admitted a 37-year-old man who was paraplegic and wheelchair bound from a service related back fracture. He came to the emergency room with a decubitus ulcer, a pressure sore, on his coccyx (tailbone). The ulcer was very deep with a 3 cm wide area of skin and soft tissue necrosis. The tissues were infected and foul smelling.

These are thankless cases. The surgery is not difficult but is unpleasant and unrewarding. The dead tissue needs to be debrided (cut away) and the wounds need to be left open to heal from the bottom up. Frequent, painful dressing changes need to be done daily for weeks.

P had been told specifically by Dr. Fletcher to take care of this patient himself. Apparently the patient was connected to the Admiral in command of the military medical school on the hospital campus, making him a minor VIP.

P, true to form, passed the case to the junior resident. Usually it would be a junior case, but P had specific instructions to the contrary. I knew this, and took the case myself. At least the junior guy would be protected.

I booked the debridement for the next morning. Just as I finished and was escorting the patient to the recovery room, Dr. Fletcher called the OR and asked to speak to P. I took the call.

"Where's Dr. P?" Fletcher asked.

"He's tied up in the ICU and couldn't do the debridement," I lied. "The case was already booked, so I went ahead with it."

Dr. Fletcher let that pass, and for a couple of days I thought he'd bought the story. I felt guilty, but the team was protected and the patient was doing as well as could be expected. Then came the message that Dr. Fletcher wanted to speak to me.

At three on the dot, Dr. Fletcher opened the door to his office and waved me inside. He sat behind his desk and I stood in front of it, not quite at attention. He told me to sit down.

"Dr. P says you took that case without his knowledge. Is that true?"

I was dumbfounded. I knew P could be a snake, but didn't think he'd throw me under the bus like this. Still, I wasn't willing to admit I'd covered for him.

"If he says so, sir. I knew he was busy and may have forgotten to tell him I was going ahead with the case."

Dr. Fletcher looked at me for a second that seemed to drag on forever. Then he said, "Dr. P has been relieved. Cut the crap. You've been covering for him for months. Now, you can stick to your story and we'll let it go, but you'll be held back until the investigation into his behavior is finished. That may jeopardize your graduation from this program. Or you can tell me what really happened and you will then take P's place as Chief Resident on Gold and on Blue next rotation until you start your own chief year. You'll miss your Red rotation this year but will start on Red for the first rotation of your final year."

I came clean with him, admitting that P had told the junior resident to do the debridement and that I'd been carrying most of the load on Gold for the past three months. I felt both relieved and guilty as I did so. It's hard to explain, but I had a strong feeling that despite P's problems, he'd been my Chief, part of my team, and I was betraying a trust by revealing his failures.

Dr. Fletcher seemed to understand my feelings. He thanked me and then said, "Loyalty to a teammate is a good thing, but it can be taken too far. You covered for P when you knew it was wrong. I know you're a better doctor than that. Which is why you'll be taking over Gold service. Now go and get ready for preop. You'll be presenting P's cases."

I went, the weight of Dr. Fletcher's confidence feeling heavier than my shame at lying to him

Getting Married, Sort Of

I met my wife on the wards at Bethesda Naval Hospital during my surgical residency. She was a Navy nurse and it was definitely NOT love at first sight. She says I insulted her the first time I spoke to her. I didn't see it that way, but given my personality at the time, it's certainly possible.

Our mutual duties (she was the charge nurse on one of the main surgical floors) forced us into frequent contact and over time we came to trust one another's abilities. She was a good nurse and a no nonsense leader.

By the end of my second year, I trusted her implicitly. She would often write routine orders during the night shift rather than awaken me for it, and then shove the charts under my nose before morning rounds and say, "This is what you did last night." Of course, that meant that she trusted me as well to sign the orders. It could mean her license and a court marshal if I didn't.

By my fourth year, she'd forgotten the insult (or at least forgiven it. She's Sicilian. They never forget anything.) We started dating, and within a few months, I'd asked her to marry me and she had said yes. That surprised both of us. My first marriage had left me with a cynical view of relationships in general. She had frequently said to anyone who'd listen that she would not marry a doctor, and most especially would never marry a surgeon. Sometimes God has a delicious sense of irony.

We planned a March 1984 wedding, as it fit into the surgical rotation schedule and we could get leave together for a honeymoon. I had started to badger my detailer in July of 1983 to get orders to Guam after my residency. By September I learned that Guam would indeed be my first duty station. Everything seemed to be going according to plan.

Then on the first of November I got a form letter requesting my spouses name, rank and service number so that accompanied orders could be cut. Accompanied orders meant that we would both go to Guam, rather than me spending two years alone there. It seems we had to actually BE married by the end of November, or the orders would be solo.

We scrambled around and got the marriage license. The 18th of November was a clinic day, which meant I had an hour and a half between morning and afternoon clinics to get married. Michele was off that day so all we needed was a witness.

I dragooned my junior resident, Rick Furman, a good friend from medical school and my best man at our church wedding in March, and we rushed up to the courthouse in Rockville, Maryland. Michele met us there. She was in a short red dress. Red is the Chinese color for good luck and she didn't have a casual white dress.

We were ushered into the Justice of the Peace and he began the traditional civil ceremony. Then the pager went off.

Rick excused himself to go to the pay phone in the lobby to answer the page. This was pre-cell phone days. The JP waited until he returned. Michele and I struggled not to laugh. We weren't taking this very seriously, I'm afraid.

Three more times as the JP tried to get through the ceremony, Rick had to answer pages. By the third time, Michele was laughing out loud and had a hard time saying 'I do' with a straight face.

Finally the Justice said, "I now pronounce you man and wife. You may kiss your bride."

Michele turned her face to me and I kissed her cheek. She was wearing bright red lipstick. I hate lipstick. To this day, I won't kiss my wife if she's wearing lipstick.

The JP signed the registry, but he looked a little reluctant. I'm sure he thought this was a green card wedding. But at least we had a proper marriage to show the detailers so they would cut our accompanied orders.

Welcome to Guam

In 1984 I finished my residency and began my real career as a surgeon. Residency is like surgery with training wheels. Even though by the time you are a Chief Resident you are, for all intents, functioning independently on a day-to-day basis, you still do not have ultimate responsibility for your patients or your decisions. The Attending Surgeon on your service bears that responsibility and the degree to which he exercises it depends on your ability to do the job of a safe and dependable surgeon. You take things seriously and treat each patient as if you were solely responsible for their care, but in the back of your mind, there is the knowledge that someone is looking out for you and will step in if you look like you're about to screw up.

Once you leave the nest of the training hospital, especially for an overseas or isolated duty station, you are truly on your own.

I knew when I started my residency that I wanted to go to Guam for my first duty station as a surgeon. In those days, a surgeon finishing a Navy residency was guaranteed to go either to an aircraft carrier for a year or an overseas duty station for two years. The Navy reasoned that we already knew how to be Naval Officers and could function in the 'real Navy', whereas a new surgeon coming in from the civilian world would spend the first few months just getting oriented and recovering from culture shock.

Carrier duty was a wasted year. I'd been aboard a carrier and knew that the surgeon did very little surgery. He was there in case of war or a casualty situation but didn't operate on a regular basis. Overseas duty at least involved doing surgery. I had been to Guam with the Seabees during my duty year between internship and residency. I knew it was an overlooked plum of an assignment. I badgered my detailer shamelessly for almost a year, but I got my orders.

I had been married for less than a year when we left Bethesda and began our travels to Guam. My wife and I had had to rush our first wedding (a Justice of the Peace quickie) in order to get accompanied orders, but had gone ahead with the big church wedding a few months later for our family and friends. She was a Navy nurse and knew the drill for change of station orders. She had handled all the paperwork and packing out because as Chief

Resident, I truly had no time for such things. She had been a surgical charge nurse in command of a dozen other nurses and corpsmen and was a formidable presence in her own right. Handling a little thing like an overseas move didn't even cause her to break a sweat.

The trip across country was pleasant. We visited friends and family; dropped off our car for shipment in Alameda, California; and boarded a commercial flight to Hawaii for the first leg of our journey to Guam.

The 'adventure' began when we reached Honolulu and presented our orders to the military travel desk at Hickam Field. The Staff Sergeant on duty had no record of us. We showed him our papers again but he said, "Nope, not here. I'll kick a copy of your orders up to my LT and we'll get you on a flight in the next few days."

Few days? We had only a suitcase each and a carryon, little cash and no place to stay in Honolulu. Besides, I had a required reporting date in my orders. If I was late, I was AWOL.

Not his problem, he said, but then he did something that I appreciated for years afterward. Not because it was out of the ordinary, but because he sent us to a place that would become a haven to us for years to come.

The Hale Koa is a military owned and operated hotel on Waikiki beach, right next to the Hilton. Recreational Services operates it and its facilities are comparable to any three or four-star hotel on the beach. Room rates are based on rank and are substantially lower across the board than any commercial hotel.

We took a taxi to the hotel, expecting barracks-style accommodations and were so surprised that we asked if this was the right place. The two days and nights we spent there were a welcome break from the long flights and allowed us to adjust to the climate and pace of the islands.

After our second day, the desk clerk called our room with a message. We were to report early the next morning for a flight to Guam.

The next morning we were back at the travel desk at Hickam at 07:00. There we waited. And waited. And waited. Finally, at nearly four in the afternoon, we were taken down to the flight line to board our plane for Guam. It was an ancient Boeing 707 operated by South Pacific Island Airways under contract to the Air Force. The paint was spotted and peeling, the wings around the four jet engines were stained with soot, and the interior was old and smelled faintly of mold and disinfectant. The padding on the seats was thin and you could feel the hard springs of the seat through it. Nevertheless, it was our only choice and we were under orders.

The seven-hour flight to Guam was an ordeal. In some ways it was worse than flights I had taken in C-141's. The seat was a torture device after the first hour and the aisle was too narrow to offer much space for walking, especially when everyone else wanted to be out of his or her seat as well. My wife took it in stride, managing to sleep most of the way.

We arrived on Guam at 4:00 AM local time and were met by the general surgeon I was relieving. Bill was very happy to see us, since his household goods had been packed and shipped a week before and he was living out of a suitcase. He had arranged a room for us at the Guam Cliff Hotel, only about two blocks from the Naval Hospital.

"I'll pick you up around noon," he said. "You can rest before reporting in. I have a kid to medevac out first thing in the morning, and that will keep me busy."

"What's wrong with the child?" I asked.

"He's got pyloric stenosis. I'm sending him to Queen's Hospital in Honolulu for a pylormyotomy."

"Why not do it here?"

He looked at me as if I had a second head. "I've never done one."

"I have," I said. "Many times. Let me talk to the parents and if your anesthesiologist is willing to put the baby to sleep, I'll do it first thing."

Hypertrophic pyloric stenosis is a disease afflicting about 2.4 infants per 1000 live births. It typically develops in first-born male infants at about 4 to 6 weeks of age and is rare after 3 months. The cause is unknown. In these babies, the pyloris, a doughnut shaped ring of muscle that forms the valve at the outlet to the stomach, enlarges until it obstructs the stomach. The hallmark is persistent non- bilious vomiting after eating (i.e. there is no green color in the material vomited because all the bile is on the other side of the obstruction). The infants quickly become dehydrated and lose large amounts of electrolytes and stomach acid. Babies have little reserve and can die of dehydration in a few hours. This is why vomiting and diarrhea in newborns is a medical emergency.

The treatment is one of the most elegant and satisfying operations ever devised by the mind of man. Through a small one to two inch incision, the enlarged pylorus is delivered up onto the abdominal wall and the muscle fibers are divided taking care not to violate the inner lining of the stomach. It takes about 15 to 20 minutes and is curative. Within a few hours, the baby is feeding normally and will go on to be perfectly healthy. I love that operation. At the time, I was considering Pediatric Surgery rather than Trauma and had done perhaps twenty of these procedures in my training.

Bill called the hospital and booked the surgery for 8:00 AM, three hours from our arrival at the Cliff Hotel. To be fair to him, he had never looked at the Cliff before booking the room and was just as dismayed when he dropped us off, as we were to be there.

The exterior made the Bates Motel look inviting. The check in desk was closed and it took ten minutes for the bell we rang (per the instructions on the desk) to be answered. A sleepy Chamorro clerk showed us to our room but didn't wait as we unlocked the door. I knew we were in trouble when I turned on the lights and a cockroach as big as a Chihuahua ran under the bed. The carpet made squelching sounds as we walked on it. There were toadstools growing from the grout in the bathroom (really!). We tried to call the desk but no one answered. By this time we were too exhausted to care. Our butts were sore from those awful seats, our eyes felt like sand dunes and we could barely string two words together. I had to be in the OR in a little more than two hours. We put our suitcases on the upper shelf in the closet, the only dry area we could see, and collapsed on top of the bed in our clothes.

Two hours later, I reluctantly left my wife in the room and met Bill in front of the hotel. We went to the hospital and I met the baby's parents. They were thrilled that we were not going to send the child to Hawaii.

The surgery went well, 15 minutes from incision to closing. I stayed at the hospital for a couple of hours until the baby took his first feeding. He sucked four ounces down like he was starving, which he had been. I was just about to go back to the Cliff and try to figure out our next move (staying there was out of the question), when a nurse informed me that the C.O. wanted to see me in his office.

*Oh, crap,* I thought. I haven't been officially logged in. What I had done was technically illegal because I wasn't credentialed until I was checked into the command. I grabbed the envelope containing my orders and dashed down to the command deck.

The C.O.'s yeomen smiled at me as I rushed in and held out my orders. "No sweat, Doc," he said. "I logged you in at 06:30. Welcome aboard. Go on in, the Captain is expecting you."

I walked into the office. Captain J. was a tall man, well over six feet and very thin. He stood up and walked from behind his desk as I entered, towering over me. He shook my hand, and told me to have a seat. There were two leather-covered chairs facing the desk. I sat in one and he went back behind his desk.

"How did the operation go?" he asked.

"Fine. No difficulties and the baby is eating normally right now."

"Good. Thank you. I didn't want to medevac him but Bill insisted he needed to go. I'm glad we could keep him here."

It turned out that the Captain had been a pediatrician for most of his career before going into the command track. He understood the disease, and although he couldn't operate himself, knew it was something a general surgeon should be capable of doing. From that moment on, I could do no wrong as far as he was concerned. That turned out to be both good and bad, but it certainly helped make my job a bit easier over the next two years.

I got back to the hotel at about one in the afternoon. My wife was waiting, sitting cross-legged in the very center of the bed, as far from any part of the floor as possible. She had already checked us out, booked a room at the Hilton, and arranged for a rental car. The limousine from the Hilton was due to pick us up at 2:00 and we had dinner reservations for 6:00 that evening. Leave it to a Navy nurse to solve problems. That's one of the reasons why I fell in love with her.

First Assist

When I was a fourth year medical student, I did my first real trauma rotation at Cook County Hospital. I had been exposed to trauma as a third year during my regular surgical clerkship and liked it. I was determined to spend some time on the trauma service during my elective rotations fourth year.

July fourth weekend, I was following the trauma intern, Dr. T, around. He was new. Internships start July first and the only difference between us seemed to be the M.D. after his name. Otherwise he was as clueless as I was.

About eight in the evening, all hell broke loose. Those were the bad old days on the west side of Chicago. The gangs had made some neighborhoods no-go zones for the cops. Cops jokingly referred to the ER at County, on the corner of Harrison and Wolcott, as 'Firebase Harrison'.

There had been some kind of large-scale battle between gangbangers in Miles Square and the ambulances brought half a dozen critical patients within a few minutes of each other.

This was also in the days before close supervision of interns and residents. Usually the Chief Resident or the Third Year on trauma kept tabs on the interns and directed their activities. This day was different because the trauma unit was slammed with patients with gunshot and stab wounds.

The intern and I were told to evaluate the 'stable head injury' in Trauma Four. As we walked into the curtained off part of the ER labeled 'Four' we saw a young black man lying on his side facing us. There was a thin line of blood that had run down his neck but I saw no other sign of a head injury.

He frowned at us and said, "Are you the ones who are gonna take this thing outa my head?"

I walked closer and saw what he meant. Stuck in the back of his head, the curved end almost completely buried in his skull, was a crowbar. Protocol for impalements injuries is to leave the object in. Often the impaled object occludes the hole it has made in a major blood vessel, controlling the bleeding. Pulling it out may break that dam and cause major blood loss. Per the protocol, the patient is taken to surgery with the object in place, anesthetized and only then is it removed. We got an x-ray (this was pre-CT scan days) and called the neurosurgeon.

He arrived a few minutes later and looked at our patient and the x-ray. He called the OR and booked a craniotomy, then turned to me and said, "You might as well scrub on this one. He won't make it out of the operating room and Dr. T. is needed here"

Wait, what? Won't make it out of the OR? But he's awake and talking to us.

The neurosurgeon drew a tight circle around the tip of the crowbar on the x-ray. "This is the confluence of the venous sinuses of the brain, the superior sagittal sinus, the inferior sagittal sinus, and the transverse sinuses. All the blood the heart pumps through the brain drains through it. It's essentially a huge vein, twice the size of your thumb with walls thinner than onionskin paper and only half as strong. Once it's torn, it's almost impossible to stop the bleeding." He sighed. "Come on. You'll be first assist on this one."

I went eagerly. I think, in retrospect, I didn't really believe him when he predicted the kid would die. All I could think about was the chance to first assist on a craniotomy. Two hours and six units of blood later, the patient died, just as the neurosurgeon had predicted.

I took it badly. He'd been awake and talking when he came into the trauma center. It wasn't my first OR death, or even my first lesson in futility, but it was the first time I had scrubbed and assisted on a case where the patient died in the OR despite what were obviously the neurosurgeon's best efforts.

I didn't have the energy to change out of my bloody scrubs afterwards until the neurosurgeon came over and said, "You did a good job. You have steady hands and you didn't freak out at the sight of that much blood loss. What are your plans after medical school?"

"General Surgery at Bethesda Naval Hospital."

"Cal Thomas is Chief of Neurosurgery there. If you change your mind and want to think about neuro, have him give me a call." Then he turned and walked away. I changed and went to find Dr. T.

I never spoke to the neurosurgeon again, and although I worked under Dr. Thomas during my neurosurgery rotation three years later, I obviously didn't change my mind.

Wedding Day, Take Two

I've been reminiscing lately about my life. Writing a memoir by definition dredges up memories. Sometimes the strongest memories are those we don't drag up from the depths by effort of will, but those that surface on their own in response to a situation or a chance remark. Such was the memory of advice that was given to me on my wedding day by my Chief of Surgery.

I had not thought of J.R. in many years. He died too young (only three years older than I am right now) back in 2002. He was one of only a few people in my life who profoundly affected the course I would take. His teaching shaped the surgeon and thus the person that I would become. To me, he idealized the virtues I have sought to cultivate as a surgeon. He was not perfect, and with the perspective of years and age I am able to see many of his flaws in a more mature light. Nevertheless, his mentorship and insistence on my best effort under his instruction made me the surgeon I am today.

It began with a chance remark from a scrub tech with whom I often work. He asked if Michele, my wife, and for the past twenty years, my first assistant in the OR, would be scrubbing the case we had later that day.

I told him she would and he said, "Good. Cases go a lot smoother when she scrubs."

I already knew that and agreed with him.

He went on, "I don't know how she does it. She helps you here, she works as a Nurse Practitioner in her own office and she does your books, too, doesn't she? She sure is a busy woman."

Those remarks made me think about all of the roles she plays in my life. She is a passionate and multitalented woman and over the years we have forged a strong, intimate partnership in both our personal and professional lives.

That realization brought back the memory of the wedding day conversation with J.R. that I had all but forgotten. It was at our second wedding, the big traditional affair at the Navy Chapel – mess dress uniforms, white dress, swords, the whole nine yards. We were at the reception afterward. The traditional dances and toasts were done and Michele and I were mingling with our guests, moving from table to table spending time with our friends and family.

We had become separated for a few minutes as Michele stopped to talk with some friends from college. I found J.R sitting by himself. He shook my hand and congratulated me as I sat down next to him, welcoming the chance to get off of sore feet.

"Dr. Glass and I had a running bet about how long it would take you to wise up and ask that girl to marry you," he said. "Glass won."

"Did he take the short or the long bet," I asked.

"Long. The whole department knew you two were an item at least a month before the August Hail and Farwell," he said, referring to the first departmental function Michele and I had attended as a couple.

He watched Michele laughing with her girlfriends for a moment, and then said, "I hope you understand what an asset she is for you."

That surprised me. I hadn't heard things put quite that way. "I do, sir," I said.

He gave me that scornful look that I knew so well from M&M conference. "No you don't. No one who's developed your skills at your age could understand that." He looked across the room to where his own wife was talking with some of the junior residents. "I know I didn't. Treat her well, encourage her, and someday you will."

Thirty years later I am beginning to understand, and it keeps me looking forward to the next thirty years

## The Bishop's Blessing

It was a rainy afternoon on Guam in late 1985. Of course, saying it was raining on Guam is like saying the Sahara is dry. Rain is the natural state on Guam. There are two seasons, the wet season from December to April when it never stops raining and the 'dry season' from April through November when it merely rains every day.

I was in the surgery clinic at the Navy Hospital doing paperwork. It was almost 17:00 and I was considering heading for home when my pager beeped. I looked at the number displayed on the tiny screen (no text in those days, just a phone number). I recognized the Emergency Room number and called promptly.

The petty officer who answered sounded stressed. He said the ER doctor was with a motorcycle crash patient and needed me right away.

I hurried downstairs. I found Dave Reed, the GMO on ER duty that day, standing at the bedside of a young man. The patient was obviously military (the haircut and the green fatigues were a dead giveaway) and was almost as pale as the white sheets on which he lay.

Dave gave me a quick summary. The patient had been riding his motorcycle toward Agana Heights, heading home after getting off duty, when he was forced off the road by a car trying to make an illegal pass. The motorcycle slid off the shoulder and onto the well-tended lawn that bordered it in that location. He might have been able to lay the bike down in the grass, but he hit a large sign the 'clotheslined' him – swept him off the bike like hitting a clothesline stretched across his path.

He was hypotensive in the field and his pressure wasn't responding to the two liters of saline Dave had already given.

Just as Dave finished speaking, the x-ray technician stepped out of the darkroom and put the patient's chest film up on the lighted viewbox. Dave swore softly. The x-ray showed a chest full of blood. The left side was completely white, no visible lung, and the right was hazy with a layer of brighter white at the base.

I called for chest tubes and a suction canister. Just as I got the first tube into his left chest, his blood pressure went away and his heart fibrillated. I called for the thoracotomy tray.

Even then, we knew that ER thoracotomy in blunt trauma never worked. Mortality was 100% in every study. But I had instituted a policy as Chief of Surgery that we would open the chest of every trauma death in the ER. My reasoning was that we wouldn't make anyone MORE dead, and if we did it often, it would be routine if we ever had a case where it might work. This had been demonstrated several months earlier when my colleague, the only other general surgeon at the hospital, had opened the chest of a woman who had been stabbed in the heart and was able to suture the hole and resuscitate her. One save in twelve thoracotomies.

The team produced the instruments rapidly and smoothly. We'd practiced this. I opened his chest through the fifth rib space and collapsed his lung. His aorta was torn at the ligament that attached it to his spine, a common deceleration injury. I got a clamp across the tear and stopped the bleeding.

"I've got a heartbeat," Dave shouted. I could see the heart contracting. We pushed more saline and raced to the OR.

In surgery, I mobilized the two torn ends. They were surprisingly clean and intact rather than the usual shredding that occurs in these injuries. We had no vascular graft material so I sutured the two ends together. That usually doesn't work because they are frequently irregular and shredded and the suture line is under tension. In this patient the aorta was a bit redundant, a lucky variation on normal anatomy that gave me enough length to sew without tension on my stitching.

The repair took almost two hours. I'm not a vascular surgeon and had only seen this procedure a couple of times (and had never done one).

Meanwhile, the anesthesiologist had called the blood bank, which in turn called our 'walking reserve supply' – the Marines from the base a few miles away. They came in a bus, thirty of them, all with O negative blood, and donated. We were pushing fresh whole blood still warm from the donor into my patient to keep up with what he was losing.

He survived the operation and went to our four-bed ICU. I was worried about his anastomosis (the suture line) and about the ischemia time – the amount of time his kidneys and other organs had been without effective blood supply. I sat at his bedside all night watching the monitors and following his pressure and urine output.

I even placed a long distance call to E. Stanley Crawford, a vascular surgeon and a Professor of Surgery at Baylor. Dr. Crawford was a Navy Reservist who had been through a few months earlier on an educational program the Navy ran for the Pacific Command hospitals. Eminent physicians who were in the reserves came and lectured for a day at each hospital and then socialized with us isolated surgeons. It gave them their two weeks active duty and let them travel the Far East. Dr. Crawford had served in Viet Nam and had invited us to call him if we had clinical questions. I took him up on the offer.

I was slightly surprised when he answered the phone himself and even remembered me. I presented the case to him and gave him the patient's latest vitals and urine output.

"I'm worried about the ischemia time," I said. "He may go into renal failure and we don't have dialysis out here. I'm also worried about the suture line. Direct repairs are risky, but I didn't have any graft available."

Dr. Crawford was a good ol' boy at heart. "Well, I'll tell ya, son," he drawled. "Down here in Texas we just cross clamp and sew like hell. That ol' boy will do fine. Just keep up with the fluids if he starts to pee like a racehorse. He's more likely to have salt wasting than renal failure."

Sure enough, twenty-four hours after surgery, his urine output jumped up and I had to play catch-up for a few days. A week later, he walked out of the hospital.

I was proud of myself, but puzzled. All the books and studies, all my training, told me that survival after thoracotomy for blunt trauma was almost zero. Yes, there were isolated reports of single survivors. But I had no illusions that our little Navy Hospital was good enough to beat the odds.

Then the patient told me what had happened after he hit the sign. The lawn he ran his motorcycle onto was in front of the residence of the Archbishop of Guam and the sign he had hit pointed out the entrance to the parking area. Just after the accident and before the medics arrived, the Archbishop himself came out of his home and knelt beside my patient, praying for his recovery and blessing him with holy water and oil. The patient was a Catholic and believed the Archbishop's blessing had been the thing that allowed him to beat the odds. I am not a believer in modern day miracles, but in this case, I'm willing to make an exception.

Brothers and Sisters

She was sixteen years old, a backseat passenger in a rollover car crash. The driver died at the scene and the front seat passenger lay in the trauma bay opposite hers. She was awake and alert and very intoxicated. Her right leg was broken between the knee and ankle, but otherwise she had no major injuries.

The other passenger from the car, an eighteen-year-old boy, lay still, his head bleeding from a long laceration and his left pupil enlarged to twice the size of the right, a sign of a major brain injury. The girl alternated between sobbing and laughing uncontrollably.

We quickly sent the head injured boy to the CT scan and moved the girl to the observation area. She calmed down and seemed rational. She asked for her cell phone so she could call her family.

The orthopedic surgeon came and looked at her leg, ordered a splint and called the operating room to book her for surgery. She called a friend on her cell phone.

About thirty minutes later, an older guy showed up. He looked to be in his late twenties. He wore black jeans and a sleeveless black t-shirt. His arms were covered with Aztec themed tattoos. Two teardrops were tattooed below his left eye, a double five-year prison term. His black hair was pulled back in a tight ponytail. His body language and dark eyes broadcast aggression.

"Where's my sister?" he demanded. The trauma nurse pointed to the curtained observation area where the girl lay. He started that way.

"Can I help you?" I asked, standing up from the chair where I'd been writing orders.

"You the Doctor?" he asked.

"I'm the Trauma Surgeon tonight," I said.

"What happened to my sister?"

I explained that she had been in an accident, that her leg was broken and that she'd need surgery to fix it. I hadn't found any other injuries.

He listed, his fists clenching and unclenching.

What was this guy's problem, I wondered. I almost told the nurse to call security, but he closed his eyes and took a deep breath, visibly controlling himself.

"She'll be all right, though?"

"She'll need to be in the hospital for a few days, but should recover without any lasting problems."

He nodded. "Was she drinking?" he asked.

Uh oh, I thought. He wouldn't be happy with the answer. He seemed to sense my reluctance.

"Just tell me," He said in a slow calm voice.

"Her blood alcohol was twice the legal limit, but she wasn't driving."

"Maybe not, but she's only sixteen."

He turned and swept the curtain aside. The girl was still talking on her phone. She looked up as he stood over her bed but didn't stop her conversation. He snatched the phone away from her and shut it off.

"You're busted," he said. "No more talking to your low life friends."

"Hey," she shouted. "You can't do that."

"I can and I did. I'm in charge now. You had your fun, but I won't let you turn into your mother."

They screamed at each other along those lines for a few minutes until the girl dissolved into tears. Her brother held her shoulders for a while until she stopped crying and covered her head with a sheet, clearly done talking as well.

He stepped away and turned to me.

"Sorry to come on so hostile. I have trouble with that. I'm her legal guardian since our Mom died last year. Mom was a drunk and never gave a damn about her, anyway. I'm all she's got now."

"You'll need to sign for her surgery," I said. "Don't be too hard on her about the alcohol. Like I said, she wasn't driving."

His nostrils flared. "I'll bust her ass if she drinks again before she's 21. I'm an alcoholic, so was our mother. Dad too, I suppose, but he left before she was born. I did two nickels in Florence before I was 26. But I got sober. Been sober for three years now. I work for New Leaf as a drug and alcohol counselor. As soon as she's out of here, she's going into the teen residential program there. I can't be her counselor, but I can be her sponsor. I'll be damned if she's going to get into the same crap I did at her age. She's smart. She can be better."

He turned away and went to her side. She took his hand but still wouldn't look at him. He stayed with the gurney, holding her hand as the nurse wheeled her to the operating room.

An O.R. Tale

She was 94 years old and had been labeled demented. She was admitted through the Emergency Room because she had stopped responding to the caregivers at the assisted living center. The ER doc checked her out and found that she was again extremely hypercalcemic--her blood calcium was too high. Normal range is 8 to 10 mg/dl. Hers was 13. This wasn't her first trip for this problem. In the past two months she had been admitted three times with calcium's over 12. The Hospitalists would tune her up with saline and diuretics, treat her with Sensipar, a drug that lowers calcium, and send her out, only to have the cycle repeat. Either she wasn't taking her meds, or they weren't working to keep her stable. After all, she's demented; she may not be able to take her meds properly.

This time, the Hospitalist who admitted her was a friend of mine. She's an Internist who is old enough to remember the days before DRG's and 'best practice guidelines'. Those guidelines say that for patients over 80, the best management for hypercalcemia is medication. Rather than simply follow the guideline. She worked the patient for hyperparathyroidism.

The parathyroid glands control calcium in the body. Most people have four glands, two on each side of the neck. Once in a while, one of those glands will stop responding to the feedback mechanisms that control the production of parathyroid hormone (PTH). It then becomes an adenoma, a benign tumor that keeps churning out PTH, no matter what the calcium--a condition called hyperparathyroidism.

The old lady's PTH was 380, over ten times normal. And her parathyroid scan, a nuclear medicine study, showed a probable adenoma on the right side. So my friend the internist called me. My first response was 'You've got to be kidding'. Did she really expect me to operate on the woman? When I first saw the patient, she could barely put two words together and those didn't make sense. She was so thin and frail a strong wind would blow her away. And yet, my friend insisted that her mind seemed clearer when her calcium was below 10 and her family was in favor of either surgery or completely withdrawing care and letting her go. So I reluctantly agreed.

We went to surgery. I did a focused operation on the right

and removed one of the biggest parathyroid adenomas I have ever seen. Her PTH went from 380 preop to 36 in the recovery room and ultimately fell to 16. Her six hour postop calcium was 10.5 and she did surprisingly well with the anesthesia. I felt pretty good about it.

When I went into her room the next morning, I thought I was in the wrong place. In bed was a bright, animated elderly woman happily eating oatmeal. Her first statement to me was 'When can I go home? I have things to do.' She was a totally different woman. One of the effects of hypercalcemia is mental depression that can simulate dementia. It's called metabolic encephalopathy and had been the problem all along. Not only did we fix her high calcium, we fixed her brain, too.

Happy ending, right? So I go out and get her chart, feeling on top of the world. I open the chart and find the dreaded Green Sheet: a missive from the Medicare case manager. 'Dear Doctor, Best practice guidelines recommend medical management of hyperparathyroidism in patients over 80 years of age. Surgery is not approved treatment for patients in this age range. You must have prior authorization for surgery or payment will be denied.'

So my friend and I save this woman from spending her remaining days drooling in a corner and Medicare is going to shake its bureaucratic finger at us and refuse to pay for her care? I hate to be pessimistic (well, a little. Surgeons are natural pessimists), but I see this as a preview of where the regulation of healthcare is headed. Follow the guidelines. Forget your experience, your training, your gut. Just follow the book. It was that gut instinct that made my friend the internist work our patient up and then push me to operate on her. How long will we be able to keep that kind of intuitive thinking in medicine?

## Sphincter Blues

"One of life's underappreciated pleasures is the filling and emptying of one's hollow viscus." --- attributed to Samuel Johnson, but maybe not.

Admit it, we all love filling our tummies, that much is obvious. But isn't a good bowel movement also a pleasurable sensation? Yes, it's inconvenient and we're taught from childhood that it's somehow nasty and not to be talked about. If you're honest with yourself, though, you'll admit that the time you get to spend sitting by yourself in the bathroom getting rid of what your digestive system is casting off can be a pleasant experience.

Our fecal continence, being able to hold everything in until the time is right, is a complex system integrating both voluntary and involuntary muscles, sensory nerves, and some of the densest collections of touch receptors in the entire body. There are more pressure and temperature receptors in the anal skin than in the fingertips.

An old joke tells of a Hand Surgeon and a Colon Surgeon debating the relative importance of their areas of specialization. The Hand Surgeon waxes poetic about how hands can do everything from hard labor to playing a sonata to gently comforting a crying baby. The Colon Surgeon then has the Hand guy cup his hands. The Colon guy then fills them with his dinner – roast beef chunks, mashed potatoes and gravy. Then he tells him, "Now open your fingers and just let gas through." That's what our anal sphincters do every day.

Sometimes, surgeons like me are forced to pervert this natural process by the creation of a colostomy or ileostomy, pulling the intestine through the abdominal wall and draining it into a bag. Patients facing this procedure express worries about things like odor, inconvenience and social concerns (everyone will know about it). In fact, with a well-constructed stoma and modern low profile appliances, none of these concerns are significant problems. For many, the stoma is a temporary problem. It can be closed in a few weeks to a few months. For others, it is a permanent fixture to which they must adapt.

In the past ten days I've closed colostomies for two patients. Neither was of my creation. No surgeon likes to inherit someone else's surgical problem, but circumstances sometimes require it. One patient came to me because of a change in insurance (thank you, Affordable Care Act). The other had his colostomy done when he was unlucky enough to be out of state when he got his diverticulitis. Both did well postop and I should see them in follow up in the office soon.

One thing I hear frequently from patients who have lived for a while with a colostomy and then had it successfully closed, is how much they missed the sensation of having a good bowel movement. Truly one of life's underappreciated pleasures.

Dancing in the OR

I was not having a good morning. I had just come off Trauma call – a difficult 24hr shift that was finally behind me. I had finished a long week of rounding on the Trauma Service and had turned the patients over to Sid, who would be the rounding Doc for the coming week. All I really wanted to do was to go home and sleep. Instead, I was in the operating room struggling through a laparoscopic cholecystectomy on a hot gallbladder.

The night had been particularly difficult because we'd had two deaths during the shift, both young people in a rollover car crash up on the Beeline Highway. One was dead at the scene, but the medics had transported her anyway, doing CPR all the way because she was just sixteen and had no external signs of injury. The x-ray we did in the trauma bay told why. She'd suffered an atlanto-axial dislocation. Her neck had been stretched or distracted during the accident, separating her head from the first cervical vertebra – essentially an internal decapitation. Immediately fatal most of the time.

The other patient, an eighteen-year-old boy was alive when he arrived but lost his vitals within a few minutes. We worked on him for almost an hour, but never even got him stable enough to go to the operating room.

I had to talk to two families and tell them that their children were dead. I don't do that conversation well. One of my friends, herself a trauma surgeon, seems to know just what to say to families in these situations. She is quiet and calm, but her compassion and empathy for the loved ones of the patient comes through clearly. I have no words of comfort to give, no particular way to ease that blow. I tend to be very matter of fact and clinical when giving that kind of news and I'm sure I come across as cold and unfeeling. It leaves me feeling both inadequate and guilty for not being able to do more.

So, I was in a foul mood when I started the gall bladder surgery. The procedure was more difficult than expected. The gallbladder was thickened and inflamed and the anatomy wasn't clear. I struggled and sweated and swore for almost an hour before I could identify the critical structures and safely get the gallbladder out.

I've written before about the Dance, that relationship between a surgeon and an assistant that keeps an operation flowing smoothly. I was definitely a half step off that morning. Michele did her best to keep up, but in the end, the operation was more of a slog through mud than a smooth dance.

I was not happy with my performance and it sharpened the feeling of incompetence brought on by the previous night's events. At one point in the surgery I even shouted at the circulating nurse to 'turn off the damn music' so I could relay instructions to Michele and our surgical tech. We usually play music in the OR during a case. The hospital computer can pull Pandora and by unspoken agreement the circulator picks the music unless someone else strongly objects. That morning it was Motown. I don't mind Motown, but it isn't my favorite and that morning it got on my nerves.

I finished the case and left Michele to close the small laparoscopic incisions. I stripped off my gown and gloves and as I left the room, I heard the volume crank up on the radio, blasting Diana Ross and the Supremes as the door closed behind me.

By the time I reached the OR control desk, I was calmer. I noticed several techs standing around the desk watching one of the monitors that let the charge nurse observe what was happening in the operating rooms. I looked up to see my wife and LaVera, the scrub tech, dancing to the music of 'Stop In The Name Of Love', including all of the Supremes' signature moves. I smiled for the first time that morning.

Women In Surgery

A few years ago, the Bulletin of the American College of Surgeons contained the text of a speech delivered by Nina Totenberg at the Olga M Jonasson symposium in Chicago. This was the keynote speech entitled 'Women in the Professions'. My first thought was 'What does Nina Totenberg know about surgery?' But the talk isn't about women in surgery *per se,* but rather women in all of the professions. To be sure, she has a very East Coast/academic centered view of a surgeon's life, and no clue about life in the trenches out here in fly-over country, but she tries to convey her message.

It's an interesting, if superficial discussion of the increased role of women in all professions. She talks about law, business, and surgery. Dr. Olga Jonasson figures prominently in the talk as a pioneer who helped forward the cause of women in surgery.

With all due respect to Ms. Totenberg, I think she missed a key point that motivated Dr. Jonasson, and many of the other female surgeons she cites. Dr. Jonasson was one of my mentors. I was a lowly medical student at the University of Illinois when she was the Chair at Cook County. She was a force of nature, the stuff of medical student nightmares. She insisted on excellence and would accept nothing short of your best efforts.

I also knew Dr. Katherine Anderson when she was the assistant Chairman at Washington National Children's Medical Center. At that time, I was a surgical resident on my pediatric surgery rotation. Barbara Bass was a fellow resident from a different program during my tenure there. Dr. Anderson was physically and temperamentally very different from Dr. Jonasson, but she, too, insisted that we strive for nothing less than excellence every day.

This is the drive behind all of these female surgeons, the drive to excel. Not because as women they had to be better than their male colleagues, but because it was simply a part of their personalities. They were/are incapable of doing anything less.

This drive is not gender specific. It is inherent in anyone who spends a lifetime becoming very good at what they do.

My experience with women in surgery hasn't been much different than with men. The good ones share the same trait that made Dr. Jonasson a great surgeon and teacher. And for the same reason, they command respect from other surgeons. For me, that respect is earned by their demonstrated competence at their craft and their dedication to improving it.

I'd be foolish to say that sexism and prejudice don't still exist in surgery. But the coin that buys respect from surgeons is competence. In my experience, for most surgeons, competence trumps gender, race, religion, or any of the other artificial divisions people place on one another.

Dr. Jonasson, Dr. Anderson, Dr. Bass, all have done much to further the acceptance of women in the surgical profession, but they did so by setting the bar high for all surgeons and then leaping over it themselves.

Breast Cancer Reflections

In the past week, I have diagnosed three new patients with breast cancer. One was pretty obvious from the size and feel of the breast mass and needed only a fine needle aspiration to confirm it. She is old and frail and palliative treatment is all we have recommended.

The other two were good examples of how we find and evaluate this disease in the 21st century.

When I first started in my surgical training, breast cancer was a simple disease to treat, at least for the surgeon. Usually there was a palpable lump in the breast that had prompted the referral to surgery. You scheduled a biopsy, and counseled the patient that the lump would be frozen and examined in the lab immediately, and if it were cancer, we would proceed immediately to a mastectomy. That was basically the only effective treatment for the disease and many women had to deal with the fear and uncertainty of going under anesthesia without knowing whether they would wake up with a breast.

Even in 1978, this was outmoded therapy. We at least knew that immediate mastectomy wasn't necessary. You could do the biopsy; wait for the final pathology report, and then schedule definitive surgery a week or more later. Just about that same time, reports of breast sparing surgery in conjunction with radiation were beginning to come out. The NSABP trials of the early 1980's soon established this as standard therapy. Mastectomy still had its place, but when possible, lumpectomy and radiation were the preferred mode of treatment.

About the same time, routine mammography screening became the standard of care. Despite some recent (and very flawed) studies questioning its value, mammography for women over fifty has been clearly demonstrated to improve outcomes and save lives (about 1 per 1,000 intentions to treat).

The combination of accurate mammography, early detection and intent to preserve the breast has resulted in the current approach to breast cancer which includes mammographic detection of tumors before they can be felt on exam, radiologic guided core biopsy (large bore needle biopsy) of the suspicious lesion and then lumpectomy with clear margins and lymph node sampling as the first and often only surgical procedure.

My other two patients recently fell into the latter category. Both had suspicious mammograms. One had a core biopsy that showed infiltrating ductal cancer. I have scheduled her to undergo a lumpectomy and sentinel lymph node biopsy (taking the node in the armpit most likely to harbor cancer) and then go on to radiation treatment. Chemotherapy is an independent decision based on tumor genetics and nodal status and I don't even try to predict that anymore. There are so many variations that a true specialist (ie an oncologist) is needed to sort them out.

The third patient had a much more complex problem. To begin with she had cosmetic breast implants done several years ago. Implants, especially modern ones, don't interfere with digital mammography, but may complicate biopsy if the lesion is too close to the implant. That was the case here. The suspicious area was right on top of the silicone implant and the risk of rupturing the implant with the core needle was too great. An open surgical biopsy was required. Fingers are more sensitive than needles and I was able get the tissue out without injuring the prosthesis. Unfortunately, the biopsy showed cancer, and I may not have cleared the margin and we will still have to come back for the lymph nodes. To complicate matters further, she has a history of lymphoma and had chest radiation for it twenty years earlier. There's a limit to how much radiation a breast or chest wall can take in a lifetime, and she was not able to have radiation treatment to the breast tumor. The implant would have to be removed in any event. (Radiation and silicone don't get along well). Her only option is a mastectomy. Even with that, her prognosis is good. The tumor is early, and has favorable genetics and biochemistry. And she can pursue later reconstruction if her lymph nodes are clear of tumor.

Treatment options for breast cancer have exploded over the past five years. The overall survival of breast cancer patients is up 40% since the 1970's. Some of that reflects earlier detection, but much is due to better treatments and better understanding of tumor biology. Women still die of breast cancer. Not all cancers can be cured, but many can be controlled for long periods of time with acceptable quality of life. We are rapidly approaching a time where breast cancer will be regarded as a chronic disease that people live with, much like COPD or diabetes.

Boondoggle

There were only two women out of fourteen new doctors in my intern group at Bethesda Naval Hospital. Dr. Patricia G. was a bit older than the rest of us, having been a nurse for several years before going to medical school. She was married to a Marine who was stationed at the Pentagon, and she was three months pregnant at the start of our intern year. The rest of us didn't have much in common with her. The other woman was Dr. Peggy P.. Peggy was a dark haired beauty. She turned heads wherever she went, even dressed in scrubs and a lab coat. She was bubbly and terminally cheerful. She wanted to be a Pediatrician. She was a very smart girl but came across as a scatterbrained ditz. By the third or fourth month of our internship, most of us had figured out that the ditz act was a defense and that Peggy was a good intern and a good friend. Most of the single guys had tried to date her at one time or another, but she avoided any serious relationships.

In early December of that year the Navy took the whole intern class on a three-day boondoggle to tour the Naval Flight Training Command in Pensacola, Florida and the Naval Diving Command in nearby Panama City. They flew us down on a military transport, put us up in the Visiting Officers Mess and showed us around the flight training and dive training centers.

The idea of this dog-and-pony show was to convince us to sign up for Flight Surgeon or Undersea Medical Officer training. Both were nine-month training schools and came with a two-year fleet assignment before we could apply for Residency. The advantage was better pay and either flight training (you got your wings and qualified for flight pay) or SCUBA and hardhat dive training (again with dive pay differential).

Thirteen of us flew down to Florida on Thursday; Patricia was due to deliver any day and was excused from the trip. After check-in and an orientation briefing, we spent Friday at the dive center and Saturday at the flight-training center. We got to ride in a T-32, jump off a 30-foot tower, and ride the helo-dunker.

Saturday night was free time and we went out to sample the nightlife in Pensacola. We'd been working non-stop for six months, covering every-other to every-third-night call. We were ready to cut loose.

My memories of that night are a little fuzzy. I know that six of us were asked to leave an oyster bar early in the evening because we managed to consume all the oysters they had in stock. I remember trying a boilermaker for the first time and slow dancing with Peggy to Chicago's 'As Time Goes By'. We closed down a bar at 01:30 and several of us were in a rented car looking for someplace to eat. With me were Ben, Wink, Don and, of course, Peggy.

We didn't find an open eatery and Peggy suddenly said, "Why don't we go to my parents' house. They live near the base and won't mind if we drop by."

It occurred to me that they must be pretty laid-back parents if they wouldn't mind a bunch of half-drunk sailors dropping in at 2 AM, but Peggy was sure it would be cool.

We parked in the driveway and Peggy used a key she found under a rock in the yard to open the door. She led us to the kitchen and started pulling stuff out of the refrigerator.

I was sitting on a kitchen stool near the back door and could see down a short hallway that apparently led to the rest of the house. I saw the hall light come on and watched a middle-aged man walk slowly down the hallway, tying the belt of a flannel bathrobe.

Peggy noticed him as soon as he entered the kitchen. "

Hi, Daddy," she said. "These are my friends from the internship." She introduced us, giving her father's name only as Jack. Jack didn't smile and while he shook hands with us cordially, it was clear from his face he was both accustomed to Peggy bringing friends home in the wee hours of the morning and at the same time not very happy about it.

"Don't leave a mess for your mother to clean up in the morning," he told his daughter, and then left us to go back to bed.

We really tried to be quiet as we made omelets and toast, but we were half drunk and there was a lot of pot banging, laughing, and shushing of one another.

We got back to the VOQ by 03:30 and grabbed about three hour of sleep before rolling out for a 07:00 muster.

That morning, the helicoptered us out to the USS Essex, an old aircraft carrier that was the training platform for teaching pilots carrier landings. We watched flight operations, toured the sickbay, and then were taken to the wardroom for lunch. The C.O. of the ship talked with us about carrier ops and then announced that the Admiral in command of the base was aboard and would speak to us after lunch.

The food was surprisingly good and only one or two of us had any symptoms of seasickness. When we had finished eating, the C.O. stood and walked to the hatch leading to the main deck. He opened it and turned saying in a loud voice, "Attention on deck. Admiral John P. arriving."

Ben was next to me and we exchanged oh-shit looks. "Couldn't be," he whispered.

The Admiral looked a lot more impressive with all that gold on his shoulder boards than he had in a flannel bathrobe, but there was no question that he was Peggy's 'Daddy'. As if in confirmation, Peggy smiled and finger waved at him. He returned her smile with a short nod.

He came near our table as he approached the front of the wardroom and said softly as he passed, "Did you boys enjoy yourselves last night?"

I had an inkling that applying for flight surgeon school at Pensacola would not be a wise career move for me.

As it was, I spent my operational year after internship with a Construction Battalion on Diego Garcia, way out in the Indian Ocean. Ben ended up in a clinic in Reykjavik, Iceland, Wink on an LST out of Subic Bay in the Philippines, and Don was sent to the Naval Support Facility in Adak, Alaska. I can't be sure, but I suspect Admiral P. may have influenced out orders.

Peggy went directly into a Pediatric residency. The last I heard from her, she'd married a Flight Surgeon, had two kids, and was living happily near her parents' retirement home in Mayport, Florida.

Observations From the Trauma Service

1) "Only two things are infinite: the Universe and Human Stupidity. And science isn't sure about the Universe." Albert Einstein

2) "There is no body cavity that can't be reached with an 18 gauge needle and a strong right arm." Samuel Shem in his book, THE HOUSE OF GOD, 1978; often quoted by Ted 'the Buckaroo' Buck, MD, Bethesda Naval Hospital, 1980-1984

3) Never run to a gunshot wound to the head. The patient will either survive without you, or won't survive with you.

4) Think organ donation. The life you save may not be the one in the trauma bay.

5) Dead is dead. Pulseless in the field means pulseless in the trauma bay.

6) The patients who tell you they have a high pain tolerance will require inordinate amounts of narcotic to control their pain.

7) Any patient with allergies to more than three classes of drugs is crazy until proven otherwise.

8) Tattoo to tooth ratio= #of tattoos / #of intact teeth. The probability of being a trauma patient is directly proportional to this ratio.

9) There are no victims. (10% error rate in this statement.)

10) Adrenaline is a great antidote to fatigue. It is also addictive.

11) A shower and clean socks have the same restorative capacity as two hours of sleep. Shaving, for some reason, does not.

12) Respect the surgeon who is good at getting out of trouble. There is great value in 'been there, done that'.

13) All radiologists lie. Treat the patient, not the x-ray.

14) Isolated head injury does not cause shock. If your comatose patient is in shock, he's bleeding in his belly until proven otherwise.

15) The pancreas is hidden back there for a reason. Don't mess with it. If circumstances force you to violate this rule, a large bore drain can be your best friend.

16) Avascular planes aren't.

17) The best replacement for blood is blood. Clear fluid can buy you time but is no substitute for red cells.

18) Sometimes paramedics do the right thing for the wrong

reason. Don't bust their chops for bringing you a 'garbage' trauma.

19) There are three types of endotracheal intubation: diagnostic, therapeutic, and punitive.

20) Oxygen is good, but breathing is better.

21) The heart can't pump if the tank is empty.

22) Stick your finger in the hole. Direct pressure will control most bleeding until you can get exposure and fix the leak.

23) You either trust your hemostasis or you don't. If you don't, don't leave the operating room until you do. One never has to come back in the middle of the night to take a tie off a blood vessel.

24) Job security for the trauma surgeon: There's no cure for stupid.

Residency, Then and Now

Residency training is the core of surgical education. Surgery is both an academic discipline and a manual skillset. We learn by doing, and residency, especially a surgical residency, retains many of the forms and obligations of an old fashioned apprenticeship. The top down hierarchy, the graded introduction of responsibility, the gradual advancement through procedures of increasing complexity, all would be familiar to a nineteenth century cabinet maker's apprentice.

When I was a resident . . . (It's a sure sign of old age when you start a sentence with, "Back in my day . . .") the training system was different in 1978 when I started my residency than it is today. Back then the hours were long and brutal. Interns and residents were actively discouraged from marriage or even long term relationships. Many of us who were married found that the union didn't survive the training. Long hours, a demand for total commitment and frequent night call (in my case, every third night for four years), all took a toll. It was expected that you would work until the work was done. There was no clock, no regulated workweek. There was just the service and its demands.

It was not a lifestyle for everyone. The washout rate was high in the first year. This was intentional. Interns were fair game for anyone in the hierarchy above them, which was just about everyone. (The old joke was that the only difference between a surgical intern and a cow pie was that no one went out of their way to step on a cow pie.) Those who went on to the second through fifth years were the ones who had not only survived but had made a commitment that this was the life they wanted.

What we got in return was a broad experience, an exposure to a wide variety of complex surgical problems, and a discipline that allowed us to function when tired, to think on our feet in the middle of the night and the stamina to keep going.

There was an expectation that you would take personal responsibility for the patients you operated on, even when you weren't at the bedside. This meant that you saw the progress of the patient from surgery to discharge as a continuous arc. If there were complications, you saw those too; and handled them yourself (with help and advice from the attending surgeon). The end result was a comprehensive picture, built up over the five years of training through patient after patient, of how an operation and its recovery should progress. When something deviated from that expected picture, you were better able to see it because you'd been there before.

    The training itself was a well defined, although not rigid, hierarchy. The attending was the top, but in my day he or she was a guiding presence rather than a day-to-day manager. That role belonged to the Chief Resident. He essentially made all the decisions about the care of the patients and directed the subordinates on his team to carry them out. He did most of the complex operations himself and assigned the lower complexity procedures to the rest of the team based on his assessment of their readiness. He had great autonomy, but also ultimate responsibility. If one of his team screwed up on his watch, he was expected to take the brunt of the attending's criticism and wrath. He might ream his subordinate a new one afterwards, but he didn't throw him under the bus. This was essentially a dress rehearsal for the real world. A good attending would give the Chief Resident a great deal of freedom but would always remain aware of the events on the service and would intervene when the need arose to protect a patient. When I was an intern and junior resident, I envied the Chief for his prerogative to take call from home. Only when I was a fourth year looking at my future role as Chief did I realize that the Chief Resident rarely went home. He had responsibility for his own work, but also for that of the entire team.

    I have not been involved in the training of residents for many years. What I know of modern residencies, I know only from what I read and have been told. What I do know first hand is the quality of the new surgeons coming out of the modern residency training programs.

    Changes in the traditional residency began about ten years ago in response to a famous malpractice case that hinged on a fatigued resident making an error that cost a patient her life. The New York Times took up the standard and led the charge for a change in the way residents were trained. Based on recommendations by academics studying industrial shift workers, total residency work hours were limited, as were continuous duty hours. When a second study five years later showed no effect on patient complications, further restrictions were introduced. Now residents are limited to 80 hours per week, averaged over four weeks, no more than 24 hours of continuous duty, no new patients for another 24 hours after duty and at least 10 hours of rest after call. These are strictly enforced, to the point where residents are commanded to leave the hospital during surgeries they are scrubbed for, during critical times in their patient's care, or even in the middle of taking a patient history. Hand-offs between residents or teams are supposed to inform the incoming doctors of important issues and pending interventions. Even in the best of circumstances, these hand-offs are subject to human frailty – key information is left out either because the presenting resident forgets or because emphasis is placed on some other piece of information.

The two most glaring problems this creates when residents leave training are first, that they have developed a shift mentality – they work a set number of hours and then expect to hand off to another surgeon or team. Only in academia or a large group practice does it work that way. If you are in solo practice, or in a rural setting where you are the only game in town, there is no one to hand off to. This also leads to the second and more insidious issue – a diffusion of responsibility. If one person is not ultimately responsible for the patient's care, then no one is. A committee approach to surgery doesn't work. The nature of surgery and the relationship it creates between patient and surgeon is at its best when the operating surgeon assumes total responsibility for that patient's care. He may call for help or consultation to manage things he is not trained for, but he has ultimate responsibility for seeing that care through.

The training model these days deemphasizes personal responsibility in favor of a team approach. Even Chief Residents are heavily supervised by their attending surgeons and never experience the responsibility of being the primary decision maker in a crisis.

There's no question that these changes have made the lifestyle of a surgical resident more tolerable. There is no evidence, however, that patient safety has been improved or that surgical errors have been reduced. In fact, there is some evidence that the frequent hand-offs have resulted in more errors of omission. This is inevitable when information is communicated from one person to another.

Although I have not trained residents in many years, I do see the new surgeons who are coming out of these programs. We have had three new trauma surgeons join the Trauma Team in the past few years. They were all smart, dedicated men and women, but they lacked the core of experience and toughness that my fellow residents of the old days and I had. We were already capable of functioning independently and indeed, many of us went right out of residency to busy and high volume, but isolated, duty stations. I find myself in the role of mentor and post-fellowship instructor to these young surgeons. It isn't a failing on their part. They don't have the sheer volume of operative experience that I had at their level and they have never been given ultimate responsibility for the patients under their care.  Most are capable and learn quickly, but all too often I am called to the OR by a young surgeon who looks up from the operative field with a deer-in-the-headlights stare and has no idea what to do next. Again, not their fault. They've never flown solo on a difficult case.

Dr. David Hoyt, the President of the American College of Surgeons, recognized this problem in his address to the College at his inauguration. He said, in essence, we have failed the new generations of surgeons by bowing to media and social pressure and as a result, the new surgeons who finish modern residencies are inadequately trained to assume the role of a community general surgeon. It is therefore up to us to mentor them and complete their training.

Every generation of surgeons believes that they received the best modern training possible. I remember conversations with my mentors who felt that my training lacked emphasis on chest procedures. When they trained, chest operations for tuberculosis were common. With better drugs to treat the disease, surgical treatments have been relegated to historical interest only. The same is true for my generation and surgery for ulcer disease. Better drugs and better understanding of the cause of ulcers has made most ulcer surgery unnecessary. Change is inevitable, but what changes is not.

The current philosophy of training has, in my opinion, taken a wrong turn. There needs to be a better balance between ensuring patients are not unduly harmed and giving young surgeons the depth of experience and responsibility they will need to function independently in the community. At some point, you have to take the training wheels off.

## Statistics and the Future

There are roughly 1000 general surgical residents trained each year in this country. Of those, almost 60% go on to subspecialty training such as Plastic, Cardiac, Vascular or Colon and Rectal surgery. That leaves 400 or so new General Surgeons per year. Even if all 1000 residents stayed in General Surgery, the numbers wouldn't keep up with the attrition of practicing surgeons over the next five years. The average age of the practicing General Surgeon these days is 55. It takes five or six years, depending on the program, to train a new surgeon, so the manpower shortage is going to get worse for the foreseeable future.

In the name of patient safety, residents are limited to 80 hours of work (including conferences, lectures and on call hours) per week and 24hrs continuous duty at any one time. It's supposed to protect patients from mistakes made by tired doctors. Except there is no evidence that, in the years of implementation, there has been any impact on patient care or any reduction in medical error. New errors have crept in as well because the resident who has reached his allowable time limit MUST be sent home, even in the middle of a crisis or an operation. Hand-off errors to the replacing physician are inevitable.

I'm not advocating long hours just because I did it as a resident and I regard it as some sort of right of passage. In the real world of surgical practice, there are no time limits. You are responsible for your patient in a crisis or during surgery and can only hand off that responsibility when it is absolutely safe to do so. Even then, you are liable for the actions of your colleagues when it comes to your patients. If you never learn as a resident to work smart, to keep working to a high standard even when you are tired, how do you expect to learn once the responsibility is all yours?

First Duty

It was 1979 and I was sitting in a cold, noisy cargo hold aboard a C-141. Around me were twenty other men, all new transfers to Diego Garcia or to Naval Mobile Construction Battalion 5, my new duty station. We had been airborne for almost 8 hours after leaving Bangkok and before that had flown 5 hours to Bangkok from Clark AFB in the Philippines. According to the garbled voice over the aircraft's intercom we were on final approach and this particular slice of hell was almost over.

This was my first of many flights on the venerable 'time tunnel' as the big cargo planes were called by those unfortunate enough to be passengers. The windowless holds were poorly insulated and indifferently heated. The temperature inside hovered a bit above fifty degrees, better than the outside temperature at 30,000 feet of minus 30, but still bone chilling after a few hours.

Half an hour later, the cold would have been welcome. Diego Garcia is a tiny atoll in the middle of the Indian Ocean. Eight degrees south of the equator, it is the very epitome of a tropical island. We stepped out of the still cold plane into blazing sunlight and ninety-degree heat. The humidity was a soaking 95% and there was no shade for a mile in any direction, the native palms having been clear cut for the construction of one of the longest runways in the world. After a long half hour, we were finally picked up by a trio of trucks for the three-mile trip to the Naval Support Facility and my new home.

NMCB-5 was the deployed unit responsible for new construction on the island. They had finished the runway before I arrived and were now involved in several major construction projects. There was the fuel pier, the new barracks, and the infrastructure and utilities project. I was joining them as the new battalion medical officer.

Four weeks earlier, I had finished my internship at Bethesda Naval Hospital. I wish I could say it had been a good year, but that would be a lie. I was bitter and disillusioned. My peers and I had been regarded as little more than temporary labor by most of our senior colleagues at Bethesda. Everyone knew that we'd be leaving for at least a year with an operational unit after the internship and that only a few of us would be back. The rest would serve out their obligated service time as GMO's (General Medical Officers) and leave the Navy to train in civilian programs. There was little attempt to encourage us to return and the prevailing attitude seemed to be that the only difference between a surgical intern and a cow pie was that no one went out of their way to step on a cow pie.

On top of that, my brief first marriage of just eighteen months was over. My ex had emptied the joint bank account, diverted the household goods shipment to an apartment in Chicago and, rumor had it, had moved in with an old boyfriend. I was dead broke and everything I owned was in my seabag and a footlocker.

My intention was to serve my four years, and then get a job. I would save my pay and make enough money to buy a sailboat and sail around the world. It wasn't a practical ambition, but I'd done the proper, conventional thing in order to get through college and medical school. Now, I was going to do what I wanted.

The trip to the battalion headquarters was short, but I was soaked with sweat by the time I reported to the C.O.'s office. The Captain didn't seem to notice. He shook my hand and heartily welcomed me aboard. We made some small talk about the flight, and about Bethesda, where he had been a facilities engineer in the early sixties. He handed me off to his aide, a bored looking ensign who in turn handed me off to the Chief Petty Officer at the medical facility. Chief Harders was the first indication I had that this was real and I wasn't in training any more.

"First," he said. "We need to get you into a proper uniform." I was in travel khakis and the uniform of the day was green fatigues. "We have a supply meeting with the S4 at 15:00. They've been shorting us on paper products and for the last two weeks, we haven't had an officer to stand up to that twit of an ensign over there and get us our full requisition. Then you need to talk to the Master at Arms. He has Petty Officer Race in the brig. Race is our only Public Health technician and if you don't get him out, the reefer inspection won't get done and you'll have to shut down the galley until it's certified." He smiled at the stunned look on my face. "Don't sweat the details, Doc. I'll run the clinic, you take care of the officer stuff. OK?"

Over the next two weeks, I got a crash course in running a battalion medical department. I had a budget of several thousand dollars to account for and responsibility for several hundred thousand dollars worth of equipment and supplies. I had a division of twelve corpsmen to lead, discipline, and supposedly mentor and counsel on everything from medical procedures to financial responsibility.

I quickly realized that the C.O. didn't want excuses. He didn't care that I had never done this before. If I didn't know the answer to a question, the only acceptable answer was "I'll find out, sir".

I met the rest of the officers and was put in a berthing hut with three of them. They were all Lieutenants, like me, and all company commanders in charge of several platoons of men. I found out right away that they were all really smart guys who could have been making a lot of money in the civilian world. They had good engineering educations and had been in the Navy for five or six years. They knew their jobs and did them exceptionally well. Excellence wasn't just a goal to them - it was a standard.

And they treated me as an equal. I was a division officer, after all, technically senior to them in the chain of command, even though I was totally clueless.

About a month after reporting in and just as I thought I was getting a handle on my job, the embassy crisis in Iran geared up. This was just after the Shah had been ousted and a bunch of fundamentalists took over our embassy in Tehran.

The C.O. called an all officers meeting after getting a flash message from CentCom. We were put on Defcon 3 and orders were given to prepare the battalion for mount out, which meant someone thought we might go to war.

After an hour or so of readiness reports from the various line companies, the C.O. turned to me and said, "Doc, what's our readiness plan for casualty clearing and evacuation."

Fortunately, I knew the answer (Chief Harders had spoon fed it to me just before the meeting. God bless Chief Petty Officers). That's when I stopped playing officer and really felt that I had become one.

My attitude changed after that meeting. I was determined to do the job to the utmost of my ability, just like the other officers around me. And I was determined to go back to Bethesda and complete my surgical training. If I was going to be a combat medic, then I needed the best surgical training I could get.

In the end, Command decided not to send us into the Iranian desert to build an airstrip for a rescue mission. The logistics were too daunting and the combat power too uncertain. They did load the battalion onto an LST and float us around the Horn of Africa for two weeks before standing us down.

Although we didn't actually see combat, for those two weeks, the prospect was very real and I came away with a new outlook on my job and on life in general. I was serving something greater than myself. People had counted on me to lead them in a situation that might involve life or death decisions. It was heady and humbling at the same time, and the knowledge that I could do it changed the way I looked at problems forever.

The Night Market

It's 1979, 11:00 PM (23:00) and Bossa and I are in Singapore wandering the night market in Bugis Street. The street vendors have been out since 10:00 or so, hawking everything from souvenir T-shirts to pirated cassette tapes to fake Gucci handbags. We're here for the food. The restaurants in the area close up at 10:30, and then reopen in the form of steam carts and propane powered grills in the street at 11:00. Some of the most expensive places in town come to Bugis Street and sell their signature menu dishes for a fraction of the restaurant price.

We find a likely collection of tables and take a seat. We order crispy duck, kung pao chicken and an appetizer of fung gor dumplings along with a couple of Singha beers to wash it down.

Bossa is the Supply Corps Ensign for the battalion, about four years younger than I, the worldly and wise Medical Corps Lieutenant. We've gotten a short R&R in Singapore during a flight layover from Subic Bay to Diego Garcia. Bossa is still trying to live down the incident with the briefcase full of money from the last time we were in Singapore (another story). He's trying to look worldly himself rather than gawking at the exotic market that swirls around our table.

Just about midnight, the bargirls appear, wandering and mingling through the crowd of diners, paying particular attention to westerners who look like they have money. ("Buy me drink, Sailor?") One of them catches Bossa's eye and smiles at him. She's standing across the street from us, just outside of one of the bars that cater to Australians and off duty American sailors.

Bossa nudges me and points her out. She's a bit tall for an Asian, but still only around an inch over my own five foot six. She's wearing a scarlet cheomsang, sleeveless, with a high Mandarin collar. The skirt is long but is slit along the left side up to her thigh. She's not buxom by any means but is curvy in all the right places. Her hair is cut short in a bob that frames her stunningly beautiful face. She smiles at Bossa again and begins walking toward us.

"Look, Doc! She's coming our way," Bossa whispers.
"She's a prostitute, Bossa."
"And your point would be?"
"She's only interested in your money."

"Which I have plenty of right now, so again your point would be?"

I sigh. "Dutifully warned. Use a condom. I don't want to see you at sick call with the clap. Have at it if that's what you want."

She stands in front of Bossa and says in Malay accented English, "May I join you gentlemen?"

I'm surprised. This is a more subtle approach than usual. Bossa stammers something and jumps to his feet, pulling out a chair for her. She and I exchange a brief look and she correctly decides that Bossa is the better prospect. Bossa makes the introductions. She gives her name as Jade and she shakes my hand with a light squeeze of her fingers. They are longer than I would have expected, but soft, and her nails are polished to a high shine. Bossa asks if she'd like a drink and she orders a gin fizz. Again a departure from the usual overpriced 'champagne' that the bargirls push on their naïve marks.

I sip my beer as she and Bossa get acquainted. Pretty soon they are snuggled close on his side of the table. Her hand is below the tabletop and from its position it's at least on his thigh, if not somewhere north of there. He's grinning at me. He waves to the waiter for another round and Jade has to shift her seat to allow the waiter to get past her. In that movement, the high collar of her dress gaps open a bit and I catch sight of her cricoid cartilage, the prominent Adams Apple.

Oh! I think. She catches my eye and sees the look on my face. She knows I know. She makes a kissing motion with her lips and I smile and look away. She returns her attention to Bossa and I order another beer, struggling with my conscience, struggling not to laugh out loud.

After a few more minutes, they get up and start across the street toward the bar where Jade first emerged onto the sidewalk. She gives me a smile and a wink. Bossa doesn't see that. He just grins and gives me a thumbs up.

I learned later about *kathoey* like Jade, a Thai word that means literally lady-man. They range from the equivalent of an American drag queen to true transsexuals who are waiting for their gender change operations while living full time as women.

Bossa returns a quarter of an hour later, a big grin on his face.

"Where's Jade?" I ask as innocently as possible.

"She had to go home. Sick mother or something. It's Ok. I paid her already."

"Did you two…" I leave it hanging.

"Best blowjob I ever had."

Probably the only one you ever had, I think, but keep my mouth shut.

I never told him, even when he bragged to the wardroom a few days later. I still laugh about it. I'm an evil man.

## Joe's Legs

I was a young resident on my trauma rotation, eager to do procedures and save lives, when we got a call from the paramedics. They were bringing in a man with a head injury and lower extremity paralysis.

As the resident, I ran the initial trauma evaluation. My attending was in his office, two floors up and I was supposed to call him after my initial assessment or if the patient was unstable.

When the paramedics arrived they presented the few known facts they had – the man was found down under a viaduct with a large gash on his head. He was homeless and smelled strongly of alcohol and a number of other less savory substances. He 'friends' could only tell the paramedics "Joe got hit in the head and can't move his legs".

Joe was only semiconscious. He would snore and sputter; he would arouse to shouted words or pain but only said a few nonsense words before becoming somnolent again. I considered intubating him because of his depressed level of consciousness, but he seemed to be protecting his own airway adequately and if we sedated him, we'd not be able to assess his neurologic exam.

We loaded him with IV fluids, sewed up the 15-centimeter scalp laceration, and badgered him repeatedly to move his legs. The only coherent thing he said was "Can't".

This was in the days when CT scanners were relatively new and exotic pieces of technology. Scans could take as long as 30 minutes to complete (compared to 30 seconds today) and we didn't get them on everyone. Before ordering one, I had to call my attending. I outlined the presentation and physical findings for Dr. Cochran and told him I suspected a central brain injury was responsible for Joe's paralysis, even though it was bilateral and symmetrical, an unusual way for a brain injury to present. I wanted to do a CT scan.

Dr. Cochran came down and looked Joe over. He turned to the nurse and ordered Narcan, a narcotic antagonist that can temporarily reverse the effects of drugs like heroin, codeine, morphine, etc. A few minutes later Joe opened his eyes. He was still confused and somnolent but was definitely more alert than before.

Dr. Cochran shouted at Joe in his gravelly voice, "Move your legs, sir."

Joe said, "I can't"

Dr. Cochran then asked the key question. "When was the last time you could move your legs?"

Joe said, "Oh man, I haven't moved them in five years. Not since I broke my back."

Dr. Cochran just said, "Cancel the CT." and walked out of the trauma bay.

Object lessons that I have never forgotten: 1) Just because a patient is drunk, doesn't mean he doesn't have other substances on board. Joe was also a heroin addict and Dr. Cochran had noticed the needle tracks on his arms. Narcan reversed the heroin enough to get a better history. Which leads to the second lesson: 2) Always get as complete a history as possible before ordering a bunch of hi-tech tests.

Joe sobered up and the paramedics found his wheelchair and brought it to us a couple of hours later.

Marine Green

In 1991 my Navy Reserve unit was activated for the First Gulf War. At the time, I was with the 4th Medical Battalion, 4th Fleet Service Support Group assigned to the 13th Marine Expeditionary Force. All the military jargon meant that we were Navy medical personnel assigned to support the Marine Corps. The Marines have no medical personnel; all their corpsmen and doctors are in the Navy and are on detached duty to the Corps.

We mobilized from our Reserve center in Tucson and were transported to Camp Pendleton, California for intake and assignment. Shortly before the war started, our unit had gone through a field exercise in CBW (Chemical and Biological Warfare). We were considered the local experts in CBW precautions and treatment. That didn't make us happy, since it seemed we were destined to take on that role in Kuwait before long.

I was assigned, along with several of our corpsmen, to the 2nd Tank Battalion, an armored unit that also included a half dozen AMTRAK's (Armored amphibious landing craft) and several Badger units in addition to the battalion's 14 tanks. Badgers are light all-terrain vehicles that look like the sand rails people drive across dunes for recreation. They have a crew of two – a driver and a gunner. They sometimes mount a light machine gun on the top 'rail', but more often carry a laser target designator. Their role was to scout ahead and illuminate targets with the laser so the smart bombs and munitions could home in on them.

Before joining the battalion, we all had to go through what was euphemistically called 'Combat Refresher Training'. CRT was supposed to take a bunch of Navy weenies and turn them into something that could at least pass for Marines, if one didn't look too closely.

We were in an odd position. On the one hand, the Marines knew they needed us and had great respect for the corpsmen who stood beside them in the line companies. On the other hand, we hadn't been through the Crucible and couldn't be regarded or trusted as 'real' Marines.

For two weeks, we were pushed through physical training, small unit operations training, weapons qualification and combat simulations by a Top Sergeant who seemed to love yelling at us 'squids', especially the officers. For the purpose of the training, we were essentially stripped of rank for two weeks. We were grunts, just like everyone else.

I confess I was not a good Marine. One of the basic Marine Corps dogmas is "Every man a Rifleman". I have never been a good shot with rifle or pistol. I have no fear of the weapons and nothing against using them. It just seems that my hand-eye coordination doesn't run to aiming and firing them. I barely qualified with the M16 and was hopeless with the 9mm pistol. Top yelled a lot, but it didn't help. He took me aside and with surprising patience, walked me through good firing stance and technique until even he had to admit that the 9mm was not going to be my weapon.

CRT ended with a live fire exercise in Combat Town, a cluster of concrete shell buildings, narrow streets and alleys, and pop up cardboard targets. Our mission was to clear the buildings, take out the terrorists and not hurt a group of hostages being held somewhere in the town.

Knowing my inability to hit anything with the 9mm, Top presented me with the Streetsweeper, a 12-gauge military shotgun loaded with flechette rounds. All I had to do was point it in the general direction of a target and at least some of the small triangular metal flechettes would hit it.

We started our sweep, following all of the precautions and procedures that had been drilled into us. I was on a flank and was assigned a small building to investigate and clear.

I cleared the front door and came into an empty room. There was a smaller room in the rear around a short corner formed by an interior wall.

I dropped to my knee and took a quick peek. All I saw was a figure in a headscarf holding an AK. I stuck the shotgun around the corner and pumped off three rounds. I got to my feet and started to check the room. Suddenly Top was at my elbow bellowing into the tactical net.

"Cease Fire! Cease Fire! CRT 17-91 stand down!" He turned to me. "Safe that weapon."

I cleared the chamber and clicked on the safety. Top grabbed it away from me and for a half second it looked like he was going to smack me with the butt of the gun. Instead he rechecked it and slung it over his shoulder. He then launched into a string of profanity that was both shocking in its detail and epic in its length. He went on for five minutes without repeating himself. He never insulted me directly (I was still an officer after all) but limited himself to cursing all squids and implying that they were the result of unnatural sexual acts between mentally deficient apes and dogs, or maybe it was donkeys. Things got a little muddled in the middle.

He pushed me around the corner to inspect the results of my blind shooting. The cloud of cardboard confetti was still settling. I'd gotten the terrorist all right. And also the six hostages he was guarding. Top took away my shotgun and gave me back the 9mm. I guess he figured that if I couldn't hit anything with it, at least I couldn't hurt anyone, either.

In the end, I never fired the weapon again. And even though we went to MOPP 4 (full CBW gear and precautions) three separate times on the road from Al Jabar to Kuwait City, I never saw any real combat. It's just as well. I was as likely to shoot myself as I was to hit an enemy. I was a very green Marine.

The Purple Man

Friday afternoon trauma shift and we get a call about an incoming trauma – 67 year old man restrained driver, hit from behind at high speed; brief loss of consciousness, complaining of chest and back pain.

He arrives a few minutes later, awake and alert, complaining of back pain midway between his shoulder blades. He is diaphoretic (cold clammy sweat) and says he is having a little difficulty breathing. What is immediately obvious is that his face is purple. Not the purple of a bruise or contusion, but the purple of venous congestion, like when you hold your breath and strain until you turn blue. The discoloration stops at his collarbones and he is normal to a little pale in color below that. His blood pressure is normal to a little high and his pulse is in the 80's – not terribly elevated.

Facial cyanosis in the settling of trauma is a sign of something very bad going on in the chest. It is caused by impaired venous return – blood flows into the head and face but can't get back out – and implies an obstruction in the superior vena cava. With penetrating trauma, this could be due to a wound to the cava with a clot occluding it. In blunt trauma it is more likely due to a big hematoma from a torn aorta pressing on the vena cava and blocking it. Even though this man's pulse and blood pressure are reasonably normal, we may be sitting on a ticking bomb.

The aorta is the main artery flowing out of the heart to the rest of the body. As it exits the heart, it sweeps up toward the neck but makes a 180-degree turn while still in the chest and then goes down along the spine toward the abdomen. That sweeping curve from upward to downward and right to left is called the arch and it gives off both right and left carotid arteries to the brain and the innominate and subclavian arteries to the right and left arms respectively. Through most of this turn, the aorta is pretty firmly fixed to the spine and muscles by tough bands of tissue. There are a couple of places where it is more mobile. One is just above the heart for about a centimeter as it leaves the annulus of the aortic valve. The other is as the aorta completes its turn and heads down toward the abdomen. At that point it is anchored by the ligamentum arteriosum, the remnant of the ductus arteriosus, a fetal structure that bypasses the lungs before they are inflated by the baby's first breath.

It is at these fixed points that the aorta can tear through shear forces caused by a sudden, violent acceleration or deceleration.

Tears of the aorta can be catastrophic and immediately (or within a minute or so) fatal, or they can be contained temporarily by the tissue surrounding the aorta. This containment may last minutes to hours, but eventually if fails as clots begin to break down and catastrophic bleeding develops.

When a patient survives to reach the trauma center with this type of injury, they are like a bomb waiting to go off. I have no way to know or predict when the containing clot will fail and so time is of the essence.

After a few quick minutes examining the patient for other injuries, we hustle him off to CT for a scan of his chest. Sure enough, he has a contained tear in the middle of the descending aorta – the part heading down to the abdomen. There is a large clot containing the tear and pressing on the cava which lives right next door.

This is a job for Cardiovascular surgery. Only a few years ago, we'd be hustling this patient off to the OR for a thoracotomy and direct repair of the injury. But not today. Today we are going to the interventional radiology suite. These injuries can often be treated with covered stent grafts, similar to the stents that are put in coronary arteries, only much bigger. The stents are cylindrical metal frames that are collapsed around a balloon. They are passed under fluoroscopy up the aorta from the groin, positioned at the tear, and then the balloon is inflated which expands the stent to its full diameter. When the balloon deflates, the stent remains in place and covers and reinforces the tear. Very high tech and slick, and it saves the patient a big cut on his chest. Once the tear is covered, the clot can be allowed to break down naturally and the cava opens up.

My purple man did well in radiology and is now being monitored in the ICU for any further signs of bleeding. I love technology.

Gallbladder Blues

I did an urgent laparoscopic cholecystectomy the other day on a young woman who called the office with a sudden worsening of her gallbladder symptoms. By the time we got her to the OR preop area, she was pale, diaphoretic (cold and sweaty) and writhing in pain. Her gallbladder was sick but not infected and she had a stone stuck tight in her cystic duct, the tube that drains the gallbladder. The stuck gallstone was probably what caused the sudden worsening of her symptoms.

I had originally seen her in the office late in July, just before I went on vacation. She was having episodes of upper abdominal pain once or twice a week and had gallstones diagnosed by ultrasound. She's an otherwise healthy thirty year old who had stones diagnosed on a pregnancy ultrasound and symptoms that started four months after the recent birth of her third child--pretty typical history. She took no prescription medications but did take a handful of herbal and vitamin supplements daily and told me she stayed away from processed foods in favor of a 'natural' diet. That should have tipped me off, but it didn't at the time.

The surgery went well, although the stone was wedged pretty tightly and I did an x-ray of the common bile duct, the main tube that drains bile from the liver, just to make sure no other rocks had gotten away from us.

When I talked to her family after surgery, her husband asked if the 'purge' had worked. I asked what he meant and he told me she had read about a gallbladder purge that was supposed to get rid of stones 'naturally' and had tried it a couple of days before. The increased pain and the stuck gallstone now made sense.

These purges are touted on various websites as a natural cure for gallstones. There are several popular ones, but they all involve a fast of several days followed by a large dose of olive oil or similar fatty meal. The idea is to make the gallbladder 'expel' the stones. These purges are at best a bad idea and at worst dangerous.

Why? First, a few words about the gallbladder and what it does. The gallbladder stores bile. When we eat, especially a meal rich in fat, the stomach and intestine secrete a hormone called cholecystokinin (CCK), which causes the gallbladder to contract and push a big slug of bile into the common bile duct and through it into the intestine. Bile acts like detergent to break fat into smaller globs that the digestive enzymes can work on. People have gallbladders because for most of human history, food supplies were unreliable. Especially for our hunter-gatherer ancestors. They might eat a large meal one day and then little or nothing the next. An organ to store bile during fasting and mobilize it in response to a meal prevented crippling diarrhea from poorly digested fat.

When we eat every day, which most people in this country do, and especially when the quantity and quality of our food doesn't vary much, the gallbladder can languish. It has nothing to do. That may be why some gallbladders form stones. We don't really know. But we do know that healthy gallbladders don't allow stones to form in the first place. So if you have gallstones, your gallbladder isn't working very well.

Purges try to take the normal physiology of the gallbladder and use it to pass the stones out into the bile duct and thence into the intestine. Sounds nice, but in practice, only small stones can pass this way. And, because the bile duct is a low pressure/low flow system, even then they often get stuck. A larger stone will just wedge itself into the duct and jam up there, causing unrelenting pain and setting up the potential for an infection or even a ruptured gallbladder.

I see five or six patients a year who come to my office or to the ER acutely ill after one of these purge attempts. Often they were referred to a website by a helpful friend, or worse, had the purge prescribed by one of those charlatans who call themselves 'Naturopathic Physicians'. Just because it's natural, doesn't make it safe. (Hemlock is a natural substance but it wasn't very good for Socrates.) You may know a friend or a friend of a friend of a friend's second cousin who 'cured' gallstones this way, but that doesn't make it a good idea.

On the other hand, it doesn't hurt my business to have a patient who is convinced in such a graphic way that they need an operation. Olive oil cocktail, anyone?

Win One, Lose One

Sometimes the magic works and sometimes it doesn't. A recent night was like that. About midnight a young woman came in with a stab wound to the groin. Paramedics said it was a five or six inch blade that entered her groin in the crease between the upper thigh and the abdomen. There was a lot of blood at the scene and her blood pressure was low--50 over nothing. There was about a pound of gauze covering the entry wound and it was saturated.

The groin is a busy place. Both the femoral artery and the femoral vein, the main vessels into and out of the leg run through the area where she'd been stabbed. The distinct crease in the groin is created by the inguinal ligament. This is a tough band of tissue about an inch thick that provides the point of attachment for all the abdominal muscles. Put a hook through it and you can lift the whole body off the ground. The vessels run under it and that makes them hard to get at.

The first rule of arterial injuries is proximal and distal control. Get the vessel above and below the injury and put your clamps on there. Trying to get control of a bleeding vessel at the site of injury is usually a losing proposition. Especially when the blood is flowing as fast as your kitchen faucet. But getting proximal control in the groin can be a challenge. Sometimes you have to get at the artery and vein from inside the abdomen.

This time, I got lucky. The injury was just below the inguinal ligament. Not enough to get good control, but enough so that by cutting the ligament, I could get at the artery and vein from the leg side and not have to open the abdomen. Lucky for her, too, because as fast as we could pump blood in, it was gushing out of the wound. Once I got a vascular loop on the vessels (a soft rubber tie that closes off the vessel without damaging it), we could catch up on the blood loss and call the vascular surgeon to do the definitive repair.

The other vascular injury patient wasn't so lucky, but that was his intent in the first place. I am always ambivalent about gunshot wounds to the head, especially when they are self-inflicted. Outcomes are rarely good. Most through and through wounds aren't survivable. Death, or at least brain death, is the norm. Even those people who survive almost never regain a quality of life near to what it was before the wound.

This was a thirty-year-old man who shot himself with a nine-millimeter pistol. Entry wound in the right temple, exit wound behind the left ear with brain matter herniating through the wound. He was hypotensive with a blood pressure of 70/40. Paramedics said he was breathing spontaneously on scene and had some purposeful movement, so we were committed to treating him as a salvageable patient.

We pumped in volume, dressed the wounds with a turban-like pressure dressing and I called the neurosurgeon. He was pretty pessimistic about the patient's chances. It was a through and through wound in a bad zone of the brain, but even so, there was donor potential to think about. It sounds cold, but Donor Network is one of our first calls in cases like this. I shipped the patient off to CT scan to assess the amount of brain injury. At that point his pressure was up to 110/70 and he was breathing on his own. His pupils were fixed and dilated and he didn't respond to pain. He was probably dead and his heart and lungs just didn't know it yet.

A few minutes later, I got a call from the CT scanner. The patient had dropped his pressure and there was massive bleeding soaking through our dressing. The scan was done, so we hustled him back to the trauma bay. I took down the dressing and found blood gushing from the exit wound behind the left ear.

First rule of bleeding control: stick your finger in the hole. I did and knew immediately that the ball game was over. I could feel the jet of bleeding from the internal carotid artery hitting my fingertip. Unlike the artery in the groin, the internal carotid at that point is encased in a boney canal. There's no way to get at it. Imagine a fire hose encased in concrete. Imagine trying to get at the hose by chipping away the concrete without making more holes in the hose. It can't be done. I could plug the hole with my finger inside his skull, but that just diverted the flow to other branches in the face and nose and all the blood started leaking from there.

I called the neurosurgeon who was looking at the scan from a remote monitor. He could see that the bullet had blown away the carotid canal in the skull and had taken out most of the frontal part of the brain as well. We decided that further efforts were a waste of time and blood products. I'd never be able to get him stable enough for transplant harvest. We stopped pumping in blood and the end came within a few minutes.

Why hadn't the bleeding been immediately obvious when he came in? I think his pressure was low enough that a clot formed in the injured carotid. Sometimes it's better if an artery is completely divided rather than slice halfway in two. A completely divided artery will contract and narrow the hole, maybe enough to allow a clot to form. The partially cut artery can't close the hole and it keeps bleeding. I think when we resuscitated this patient and pushed his pressure up to 110, it blew the clot out of the end of the artery and he started bleeding again.

Object lesson--not all bleeding can be controlled, but all bleeding stops eventually.

Traffic Cop

Sometimes, my job involves playing traffic cop, or referee, when two different specialists have competing interests in the same trauma patient. As the trauma surgeon, I have ultimate responsibility for decisions on care, even when it isn't care that I am personally delivering.

Recently we got a man in from a motorcycle accident with a complex pelvic fracture. He had what's called an open book fracture. It's a disruption of the pubic symphysis, the joint in the front of the pubic bone, as well as a disruption of the sacroiliac joint in the rear. Think of it as the splits taken to the extreme. This disrupts the plexus of blood vessels around the pelvic ring and often causes massive bleeding. It can also tear the bladder or rectum and spill their contents into the pelvis or abdomen.

The treatment for the bleeding is to reduce the fractures - pull the separated bones back together again. We can use a metal frame and screws placed into the bone through small incisions, or a simple binder around the hips. The bleeding isn't the kind you can fix with ties or sutures. It's rapid bleeding in a tight dark box with no easy ends to tie or tissue to sew. Fortunately, if you close the box, by pulling the bones together, you may create enough pressure to slow or stop the blood loss. The last thing you want to do is open that box by making an incision in the abdomen or pelvis. It's like taking the top off of a shaken up bottle of soda.

So my orthopedic colleague wants to place a binder on this gentleman and monitor him in the ICU, aggressively replacing blood and components until the bleeding is controlled. Then he can operate to fix the fractures.

But in this man we also had a ruptured bladder. Worse, the rupture was into the peritoneum, the abdominal cavity, and was bathing the intestine in urine. The treatment needed is an operation to repair the tear. But that involves opening that bloody box and releasing the pressure.

Now I have a Urologist and an Orthopedic Surgeon glaring at me, a charge nurse who wants to know if she should call the Operating Room or the ICU and a patient whose blood pressure is starting the slow slide that means we're falling behind on his volume replacement. Do we delay surgery and risk infection, sepsis, and possible death? Do we go to the operating room and repair the bladder and risk him bleeding to death by releasing the pressure keeping the blood loss down to a manageable rate? My decision, my job.

After some consideration, I decided that the risk of infection from a bladder rupture outweighed the bleeding risk. Urine itself is sterile, but it is a chemical irritant to the bowel and is a pretty effective anticoagulant. Enough urine in the pelvis and the blood won't clot anyway.

We started some bigger IV line, ones that we could pump blood through as fast as it would run through the tubing. I helped the urologist. The bleeding was alarming. The suction ran continuously making a sound like water running down a drain. The anesthesiologist did a great job. She pumped in ten units of packed red blood cells, ten units of plasma, two platelet packs and two rounds of concentrated clotting factors (called cryoprecipitate). That's on top of almost five liters of saline. We fixed the bladder and the orthopedic guys placed an external fixator - a frame to pull the pelvis together. We made a stop in the angiography suite after surgery where the radiologist embolized some big bleeders. By placing a catheter in the bleeding vessel, they can inject small plugs that block the bleeding vessels and clot them off. By the time we made it to the ICU, the patient was stable, the bladder was fixed and the pelvis was reasonably stable. He's facing a lot more surgery, but should recover.

The point of this story is that this was a team effort. A lot of different people had to do things as a team to get the result we did. I couldn't do it myself. I don't have the training to fix the bones, and although I could fix the bladder, the repair wouldn't be as good as the urologist's. He does that work every day. My primary role here, and in a lot of other, less intense traumas is to prioritize the interventions and make sure that the competing interests don't sabotage each other.

Why I Won't Fly in Helicopters

When I was a young Medical Officer in the Navy, I was assigned TAD to the *USS America*, an aircraft carrier, for a few weeks while her own surgeon was on emergency leave. TAD is Temporary Assigned Duty, basically a short-term special assignment for a specified time and purpose. What began as a two-week boondoggle off the coast of Florida in February had turned into a two-month ordeal off the coast of Norway when the surgeon I was relieving failed to return on time. I had stupidly not brought my entire seabag but only a small pack with summer uniforms and a light jacket. (In those days, I still trusted orders to be accurate. They read two weeks temporary duty and I figured I'd be back home before the ship headed north.)

The North Atlantic in February is very cold and wet. The temperatures and my lack of proper uniform kept me below deck for the entire cruise. I traveled the circuit of heated spaces – berthing to sickbay to wardroom – and never saw the sun.

About four weeks after the ship left Florida and six after I'd joined her, we got an urgent call from one of the FFG's (Fast Frigate, a small ship about the size of a WWII destroyer) in the task force. One of her crewmen had fallen from a catwalk in the engineering spaces and had possibly broken his neck. They were requesting a medevac and a physician to come over and evaluate him. I volunteered to go. I was still young and foolish and hadn't yet learned the adage that "NAVY" stands for "Never Again Volunteer Yourself". In truth, I was bored to tears. I was there only in case of surgical emergencies and as the Casualty Control officer in the event of combat. Seeing scrapes and bruises and sore throats at morning sickcall held no appeal for me.

I borrowed a flight suit and a parka from one of the air wing flight surgeons and was bundled aboard an SH-2G Seasprite helicopter for the trip over to the FFG. Fast Frigates are helo capable, barely. Landing on the pitching afterdeck of a small ship with only a few feet of clearance for the rotors is a skill that even a naïve young officer like me had to admire. The pilot made it look routine, which, for him, I suppose it was.

I was met by the ship's senior corpsman on the small flight deck. He was a very capable First Class Petty Officer with an Independent Duty rating. He filled me in on the patient's vitals and exam findings as we descended into the ship's interior. He had immobilized the man's neck with a rigid collar and they had already loaded him aboard a Stokes litter by the time I got there. A quick exam confirmed that he had severe neck pain but a neurologic exam that had puzzled the corpsman. The patient could move his legs and had normal sensation in his lower body but could not move his arms or hands and complained of burning pain in his upper extremities. With a simple spinal cord injury, you'd expect a loss of function for everything below the level of the injury. If the arms were paralyzed, everything below that level should be, too. This guy's legs and trunk were fine. Only his arms were affected.

I knew right away what was going on and filled the corpsman in. It's called central cord syndrome. Sometimes a hyperextension injury, where the head is force back violently, can pinch the spinal cord between vertebrae, or push a posterior arthritic bone spur into the cord. The pinch injures the blood vessels in the middle of the cord, cutting off or reducing blood supply to the lateral columns of nerves at the level of injury while preserving the central grey matter. In other words, a selective bruising that tends to affect the upper extremities and sensory nerves at the level of injury rather than cutting the entire cord at that level.

It's usually reversible, but it's critical to keep the blood pressure stable or even a little high to make sure the area is well perfused. The patient was reasonably stable but needed to be in the more sophisticated sickbay aboard the carrier.

The crew hauled the heavy Stokes (a rescue litter with raised sides, like an elongated metal basket) up four decks to the flight deck and we loaded him aboard the helicopter.

The flight back to the carrier was rough. A stiff headwind had come up and the small aircraft was buffeted around a bit. I am not a fan of small aircraft and was white knuckling a stanchion the whole way. The flight crew took it in stride, as if this was just routine, but that didn't calm me much.

As we made our final approach to the fantail of the carrier there was a metallic ping and the engine noise changed pitch. The first indication I had that this wasn't good was when the crew chief grabbed a stanchion himself and checked his seatbelt. A second later there was a bang and the engine cut out entirely. We were about a hundred feet up and a little aft of the fantail, over water that was barely above freezing. Survival time in that cold would be measured in seconds.

There was a weird whomping sound and the helo began to drop, fast but not in freefall. We hit hard and bounced once, but stayed on the deck of the carrier. The rear landing wheel of the little aircraft was only a few inches from the edge of the deck and the tail rotor was hanging out over the water

I managed to hold it together while the crew unloaded our patient and by the time I got him to sickbay, I no longer felt like vomiting. I was also glad I had emptied my bladder before we left the carrier. My underwear managed to soak up the little bit of urine I lost from fright and I didn't have to explain to the flight surgeon why his flight suit was wet.

I talked to the pilot afterwards. The engine had eaten some kind of flying debris and seized up. The whomping sound had been the rotors turning. The pilot had disengaged them from the engine allowing them to spin freely. The downward momentum of the falling helo had spun them, creating just enough lift to allow the pilot to reach the deck and land. It's called autorotation. He seemed to think the incident was no big deal and was more worried about the ability of the maintenance crew to fix the engine.

I have never flown on a helicopter again.

It Ain't What You Don't Know . . .

Sometimes medics do the right thing for the wrong reasons. Sometimes trauma surgeons can get misled by what they think they know. Mark Twain is credited with saying, "It ain't what you don't know that can hurt you, it's what you know that just ain't so."

A while back, I was on call on a Saturday night when we got a notification of an incoming trauma, an intoxicated 40 year old man who had fallen off a barstool and had a scalp laceration. He had a brief loss of consciousness, but it occurred before he hit his head – it seems he passed out, which is why he fell. My first thought was, why is this a trauma? But we don't get to make that judgment until the patient actually arrives and I can do an initial assessment, or primary survey.

The patient arrived a few minutes later, awake but clearly intoxicated and a bit belligerent. He was restrained, had a cervical collar on and a bulky, blood soaked gauze wrap around his head.

The medic presented the case: the man had staggered into the bar about an hour earlier and had taken a seat on one of the stools. He ordered a beer, but the bartender refused to serve him. He started to stand up, but then passed out and hit his head on the edge of the bar.

I restrained myself from asking what 'life or limb threatening injury' the patient had that made him a trauma and thanked the medic.

I introduced myself to the patient. His speech was slurred and his breath was strong enough to get you high if you stood to close to him. He smelled of other things as well, so I didn't want to do that.

His pupils were equal in size, there was no deviation in his gaze and no blood in his ears. He was speaking spontaneously and followed simple commands. He moved all of his extremities. I doubted he had a brain injury and assumed that he was just drunk and the obvious bleeding from his head injury had fooled the medics into thinking the injury was more serious than it actually was.

I began to unwrap the dressing to look at the wound and assess the bleeding. Then the nurse called out his blood pressure. It was very low, only about 80 systolic (the higher of the two numbers used to report blood pressure)

I got the wrap off and found a three-inch laceration in his forehead that was bleeding briskly. Pressure on the wound controlled the bleeding and I called for some local anesthetic and sutures. A few sutures controlled the small scalp artery and stopped the bleeding. The blood pressure stayed low.

There's an adage in trauma surgery that isolated head injury does not cause hypotension. The brainstem protects brain perfusion and head trauma, if anything tends to raise the pressure. If the injury affects the brainstem, or if the brain is being pushed into the opening in the base of the skull (herniation), then the blood pressure may go down, but by that time the patient isn't likely to survive.

I went through my primary survey, but the patient was so drunk that he barely responded, even to deep pain. Still, I didn't see any obvious injury or anything from the mechanism of injury that would explain his persistent low blood pressure.

Could he have bled so much from the scalp laceration that he was in shock?

I doubted it. The bleeding had been brisk, but not that significant. Medics and even surgeons often overestimate blood loss. 50 cc on the floor looks like a pint. It only take 5 to 8 cc to turn a gallon of water so red that you can't read newsprint through it. So I doubted that the head trauma accounted for his hypotension.

His pressure dropped even lower – into the low 70's systolic. I was puzzled, but had to do something.

"Start the red cells," I said. "Two units of 0 negative, two of FFP (fresh frozen plasma), and a 500cc saline bolus. Type and cross him for four in case we need it."

"What x-rays do you want, Bruce," the Trauma nurse asked.

"Plain chest, CT head and c-spine," I paused, a thought occurring to me. The second half of that surgical adage – 'Isolated head injury does not cause hypotension. The hypotensive patient is bleeding into his belly until proven otherwise.' "Get a CT of his abdomen and pelvis, too."

She gave me a questioning look, but put in the order.

The packed cells and plasma helped. His pressure was up into the low 100's. He went off to CT and a few minutes later, I knew why he was hypotensive. The CT of his abdomen showed a Grade 4 splenic injury.

The spleen lives in the left upper abdomen. It's about as tough as a ripe tomato with a capsule that is like the tomato skin and a center that is pulpy and full of blood. Injuries to the spleen are graded 1 through 5 based on the amount of disruption that has occurred. Grade 1 amounts to a bruise, Grade 2 may bleed into the splenic substance but not outside of the capsule, Grade 3 breaks the capsule and bleeds into the abdomen. Grade 4 and 5 refer to differing degrees of catastrophic destruction of the spleen. This guy wasn't hypotensive from his head injury, but he was bleeding into his belly.

Many lower grade splenic injuries can be managed without surgery, provided the patient remains stable. A high-grade injury, especially in an unstable patient, means a trip to the operating room.

We took him to the operating room directly from the CT scanner and I took out a spleen that was broken into four pieces and evacuated almost a liter of blood from his abdomen. Two more units of blood and another liter of saline later, he was stable and on his way to the ICU. I'd lost valuable time barking up the wrong tree and ignoring the second half of that old adage. I didn't see the clues to his abdominal bleeding because I thought I knew how he'd been injured.

It was another week before I pieced together what had happened. The patient remembered nothing about the night he came in and was no help. A fall from a barstool shouldn't cause the degree of damage he had in his spleen. But three days after he was admitted, the cops fished a Smart Car out of the East Mesa Canal, about a quarter mile from the bar where my patient had passed out. It took a couple of more days to confirm that it was his car. He had been drunk long before he drove it off the road and into the canal. He'd injured his spleen in the crash but had been able to crawl out and climb the bank, then walk to the bar before his blood pressure dropped enough to make him pass out. The puzzling thing was: why hadn't he been soaking wet?

Salt River Project, the company that operated the canal answered that at the end of the week. The canal had been drained for maintenance that day. It had been refilled about three hours after the crash, completely covering the little Smart Car.

To paraphrase Mark Twain: It ain't what you know that trips you up, it's what you think you know that just ain't so.

Strange Day at Camp Lejeune

It was uncommonly hot for early May, even in costal North Carolina. Temperatures hit the high 80's and the humidity was near 90%. It felt more like July than May. Maybe that's why events went the way they did.

I was the duty surgeon that day, a Friday. Clinic was done before noon and most of the staff had already been relieved and the duty watch set across most of the hospital. I was considering going home myself when the Emergency Room called. They had a patient with a gunshot wound to the calf. I went right over.

Despite the fact that live fire exercises were going on every day and the majority of the local population had at least one gun in the home, gunshot wounds were uncommon at the Camp Lejeune Naval Hospital. Marines take weapons safety very seriously and thoroughly investigate any firearm related incident. I was mildly surprised to be called for such an injury.

I was even more surprised when I saw the patient. He was a senior Gunnery Sergeant, the hash marks on his sleeve proclaiming 24 years of active duty. Not the kind of Marine I'd expect to be involved in an accidental shooting. He sat upright on the ER gurney, his right leg wrapped in a field dressing, the seam of his fatigue trousers already split up to the knee.

I introduced myself and took down the dressing so I could examine the wound. It was a clean through and through wound to the muscles of the lateral calf. There was little bleeding, the muscle compartments were soft and he had a good pulse in the foot. Sensation was intact and he had full mobility, with some pain inhibition, in the foot and ankle. Overall, a painful but not serious wound.

I ordered some antibiotics and a clean dressing. Then I asked, "What happened, Gunny?"

He looked away. "Accident, sir."

"I figured," I said. "But how did you get shot?"

"Will this go into the record, sir?" he asked.

"Medical records are privileged, Gunny. Hospital use only."

He sighed. "We were down on the pistol range at SOI." (School of Infantry) "The recruits were in their final 9mm quals. One of them experienced a jam in his weapon. I went down to the firing line and took the weapon from him to clear the jam. As I pulled back the slide to eject the round from the chamber, it slid out of my hand. I guess my palm was sweaty with the heat today. Anyway, the weapon discharged and a round went through my calf."

I nodded. "What's your role down at the range, Gunny?"

He looked away again. "I'm the Range Safety Officer, sir."

*Not for long,* I thought, but had the good sense to nod and keep my mouth shut.

A couple of hours later, I was on my way home and had just cleared the main gate when my pager chimed. This was before cell phones, so my choices were to drive home and call in, find a pay phone, or turn around and go back to the hospital. I chose to go back as the path of least aggravation and was glad I had. I walked into a buzz of excitement in the ER.

The GMO on ER duty flagged me down and waved me to the bedside where he was evaluating the patient.

"What have you got," I asked.

"Shrapnel wound to the abdomen," he said. "Just above the groin. He's stable but having diffuse abdominal pain. He's with Explosive Ordnance Disposal. Apparently they were trying to disarm some kind of munition when it exploded."

I checked the patient. There was a three-inch wound in the right lower quadrant of the abdomen with a small loop of bowel protruding from it. An odd black substance, like old tar, was embedded in the skin surrounding the wound. There was no doubt that we would be going to the operating room. I didn't need an x-ray to tell me that. I did need one to tell me where the shrapnel fragment was.

If bullets or shrapnel are embedded in muscle, we don't try to remove them. The body will wrap them in scar tissue and retain them harmlessly. Digging into injured muscle and tissues in order to remove metal is a waste of time and usually does more harm than good. The piece of metal that had done the damage was in the psoas muscle near the patient's right kidney.

"What happened?" I asked the patient.

"We were trying to disarm a Parrott shell by steaming out the charge in its center when it went off."

"What? A Parrott round? As in 10-pounder Parrott rifle?"

He nodded. "The Seabees working on the sewer extension at Cherry Point found it buried in a sand bank. It was still live, so they called EOD."

I was amazed. The Parrott rifled cannon was one of the most common artillery pieces of the Civil War. Used extensively by both sides, it was usually seen as a 10-pounder, 2.9 or 3-inch field gun; or a larger 20-pounder, 4-inch emplaced defensive gun. It could fire solid bolt shot, canister, or exploding shells. The typical Parrott shell was cylindrical with a crude fuse that was ignited by the heat of the gun as it was fired. The shell was of 'fractured' cast iron, hollow, with the central core filled with black powder. Fractured Iron was heated and then doused with cold water to prefracture stress lines in the shell. It made it easier for the charge to break the shell into smaller fragments that could cover a wider area. It was rare to find an intact shell; even more rare for the black powder inside it to still be volatile.

I took the EOD technician to surgery and resected a couple of different areas of the small intestine. The black stuff was indeed tar, which gave me a clue as to why the shell was still active after 123 years.

I did a little research and found out that it was likely a Navy shell, fired from a 3-inch Parrot mounted on an ironclad gunboat. The Neuse River was the site of several artillery battles between ironclads and the forts guarding the mouth of the Neuse. Navy shells were coated with a thick layer of tar to prevent water from soaking into the shell and ruining the black powder that was the explosive force of the weapon.

The shell had probably missed one of the forts and embedded itself in a sand bank, which snuffed out the fuse. And here, 123 years late, it found a target.

The EOD man did well and returned to full duty in a month. The Gunny weathered a firearms incident investigation and resumed his duties as Range Safety Officer with an object lesson and scar to show to the recruits.

How Surgeons Think, Part 1

The Hospitalists admitted a long time patient of mine just after Christmas with a bowel obstruction. He has known metastatic colon cancer and has had trouble with intermittent obstructions for some time, probably due to tumor deposits. I admitted him for the same problem just after Thanksgiving and he got better without surgery, as 80% of obstructions do. We talked at the time about surgery. The bottom line in this situation is that when the obstruction doesn't resolve or when it becomes a recurring issue, surgery is an option. With tumor you never know. You may or may not be able to fix the blockage. If the tumor is too extensive you may do an operation for no gain. I told him I would discuss it with him again if the symptoms became unbearable and he wanted to try an operation.

He went home but didn't fully recover. Every few days he'd have obstruction symptoms again. He'd stop eating for a day, get better and start back on a diet only to have trouble again several days later.

On this admission, the Internists plugged him into IV nutrition, and resolved his pain and nausea. They then dithered for five days, trying again and again to advance his diet before deciding to send him home on home IV therapy. For some reason, the Hospitalist on call New Year's Day decided to call me to see him before discharge so I could arrange to follow him in the office.

I sat down with him and laid out the options. He clearly wasn't getting better with waiting. His choices were to have surgery in hopes of relieving his blockage or do nothing and enter hospice. The options are easy to present, the choice is very hard. But up until our conversation, none of the doctors caring for him had laid the choices out clearly for him. He chose to risk the operation. I canceled his discharge and he's scheduled for Monday.

The difference in approach to this patient was very clear. From the admission five days earlier it was clear to me that he was going nowhere. No amount of time or medication would resolve the problem. A clear presentation of options was needed so that a very hard choice could be made. But someone needed to articulate those options for the patient. None of the internists could or would do that.

How Surgeons Think, Part 2

I was on trauma call recently and an unfortunate young man was brought in after being run over by a car. He was riding his bicycle home from a local pub, (blood alcohol .2) when he lost his balance and fell. He landed in the traffic lane rather than the bike lane or sidewalk and was run over by a car. The wheels went over his pelvis and abdomen. He arrived at the trauma unit in serious trouble with a nasty pelvic fracture, a dislocated hip, multiple broken ribs, a punctured lung and a distended abdomen. He was in shock and having trouble breathing and in severe pain. We quickly determined that the problem with his breathing was the hole in the lung and the resulting pneumothorax (air in the chest cavity that compresses the lung and restricts breathing). Easy to fix with a chest tube, a tube passed between the ribs into the space between the chest wall and the lung to suck the air out and reinflate the lung. Sixty seconds after placing the tube he was breathing better.

His blood pressure was still low but it responded transiently to a shot of IV fluid. Better to replace lost blood with blood, so we gave him two units of O negative. Wonderful stuff, blood. O neg is often called 'universal donor' blood because it lacks the major antigens that cause most transfusion reactions. You can give it with reasonable safety to any blood type without waiting for a cross match. The blood boosted his pressure to a safe range and bought us time.

A quick exam and a plain x-ray of the pelvis showed a complex pelvic fracture and a dislocated hip. You can lose a lot of blood into a fracture like that. It could account for his shock. But his abdomen was tender and distended and he was still having episodes of low blood pressure. He just looked like he had blood in his belly. I thought about going to CT scan, but another dip in the pressure decided the issue. We were going to the operating room.

At surgery, I found very little free blood in the abdomen. But under the colon on the left side, where the left kidney lived there was a telltale stain of bright red. The bleeding was in the space behind the intestine called the retroperitoneum. Dangerous stuff lives back there: the kidneys, the pancreas and the great vessels - the aorta and the vena cava, the largest blood vessels in the body. Bleeding back there can make a noise when it cuts loose. (Literally, turn on a faucet and listen to the sound it makes splashing into the sink. Bleeding from one of those vessels can sound like that). Surgeons say a brief prayer before entering that area.

    I opened the area where the blood was, taking care to stay close to the big vessels so that I could get control of them if I needed to. The bleeding was coming from the artery and vein that supplied the left kidney. A vascular clamp on the root of the renal artery slowed things down and bought time to dissect out the artery and vein and assess the kidney. Unfortunately, the artery had been torn off of the hilum of the kidney, the place where the vessels and the ureter enter the substance of the organ. (Imagine a kidney bean; the hilum is the dent in the side of the bean) That's not a repairable injury. I might be able to jump a graft from the aorta, but there wasn't enough blood vessel on the kidney side to sew to and the substance of the kidney around the hilum had been crushed to hamburger. No other choice really. The kidney had to come out.

    That's a hard decision to make on the fly. This was a healthy young guy with no medical problems. He had an intact right kidney and clear urine in the catheter we placed before surgery. I had the anesthesiologist give a little blue dye in the IV and within seconds the urine turned green so I knew the right kidney worked (A one shot IVP or a CT would have been better but we didn't have time and I was concerned about giving contrast) He'd survive just fine with one kidney, but taking the left one out still felt like a failure. I went ahead anyway. The rest of the procedure was routine and after closing the abdomen, we went to CT and got good pictures of the head, neck and pelvis. The right kidney is working fine. He's still sick, his lung is damaged and he has a lot of toxic byproducts from the crush injury to his muscles in his system causing problems for his heart and kidney.

    I am still second guessing the decision. It's an occupational hazard. I still believe it was the right thing to do. The interesting thing is the reaction of the various specialists who are involved. My fellow trauma surgeons listen to the description of the injury and nod and say "Good call". The intensivist (a pulmonologist, or lung specialist, by training) asks if I called in a vascular surgeon or urologist to help make the decision. I didn't. Aside from it being O-Dark-Thirty in the morning, the answers would have been the same. Why spread the pain around? The answer, of course, is spreading the responsibility. Internists are accustomed to medicine by consensus. Get multiple opinions and decide on a course of action that all agree upon. Surgeons tend to take individual responsibility for action. I may ask for input if I'm uncertain, but in the end, I'm ultimately responsible for the outcome.

     As Dr. Blalock, the father of pediatric cardiac surgery, said back in the 1940's "The mark of the surgeon is the ability to make irrevocable decisions on the basis of incomplete information."

Age and the Trauma Surgeon, Part 1

I'm nearing the end of a particularly brutal two weeks. We've been short handed on the trauma service and I've been covering both the Intensive Care Unit and the regular trauma floor for the past couple of weeks. On top of that, my regular general surgery practice has been busy with some unusually sick patients. I've been running on five or six hours of sleep a night since the first of the month and that is often broken by phone calls from the hospitals.

Twenty years ago I would have reveled in this. I love the challenge of taking care of critical patients and still believe that a doc at the bedside can make all the difference when sick patient gets in trouble. Now, I'm struggling with fatigue and frustration. I don't bounce back the way that I used to.

What's frustrating is that, while I've never been better at what I'm doing, I'm so fatigued at the end of the day that there's little left for my family or any other interests except sleep. I've said before that there is value in 'been there, done that' when it comes to surgery. I've been at this game long enough that decisions and techniques that I had to think about twenty years ago are second nature now. I don't have to think too hard about what to do in a crisis. And I've done enough operations that I can move fast when I have to in order to buy time to do thing right.

It's no different in any other specialized field. There's a popular book that proposes that it takes 100,000 hours of practice to truly master a skill. If that's so then I've mastered mine twice over. So have other people my age who have been working in a specialty for as long. We are at the top of our games, whatever they may be. But sometimes the pace of work demands a stamina that I just don't have anymore. My pathologic inability to say 'No' when asked to help out is putting me in situations where I may not be able to deliver. It hasn't happened yet, but the day is coming.

## Crosses Only Work on Vampires

I am a tolerant person when it comes to religion. My sainted wife is a devout Catholic. Me, I'm a Drunkard, a disciple of the Church of St. John Barleycorn, Scotch Rite. My wife has given up on bringing me into the Catholic Church. She says God will call me in his own time. Maybe so. If I were to join an organized church, the Catholics have a lot going for them, not the least of which is 2000 years of history. I respect any institution that's been around that long.

I also respect anyone's commitment to a belief system, religious or otherwise. I may disagree with you, but I will respect your commitment to what you believe. What I have little patience with is proselytizing. I'm happy to discuss theology (or politics; sometimes there seems little difference) with anyone, but only if there is honest give and take. Don't try to convert me under the guise of 'rational discussion'.

I occasionally encounter patients who feel compelled to ask me about my religious preferences. I usually avoid a direct answer, and if pushed, fall back on the general statement "We're a Catholic family" (which is true if you consider my wife and kids). I even have a crucifix hanging on one wall of my office, a gift from my wife.

I also have a stock answer for Jehovah's Witnesses who ask about blood transfusions. Witnesses refuse blood under any circumstances, citing some obscure Bible verses to support their belief. I tell them that I don't expect to need to give blood for their operation. As long as they sign a statement refusing blood even in life saving situations, I will go ahead with even major operations. I have issues when parents refuse to give blood to children (we have court proceedings for that) but figure adults have the right to make their own decisions, even stupid ones.

So when a recent patient made a point of telling me she was a Jehovah's Witness before I'd even had a chance to introduce myself, I was a little disconcerted. But I reassured her that it made no difference to me. A 'friend' who was there for 'support' accompanied her. Sometimes they travel in packs. We discussed her diagnosis (gallstones) and the surgery (a laparoscopic cholecystectomy). She asked the inevitable question about blood and I gave her my usual answer.

At that point the friend spoke up and asked me if I knew about alternatives to transfusion. Yes, I replied politely. I'm a trauma surgeon. I know a lot about volume expanders and fluid resuscitation. But did I know about 'blood boosters' that can be given to patients to increase their blood supply? Yes, I said, erythropoietin can do that but only over a period of days. It doesn't help much in the acute setting.

Then it got a bit weird. The friend wanted me to watch a video she had brought explaining the principals of her church and 'educating' me on the care of Jehovah's Witnesses. I told her that wasn't necessary. We were talking about a low risk operation on a healthy person. Blood transfusions were unlikely to be an issue, and even if the need arose, I would abide by my patient's wishes. She said that was good, but what about me? Did I know about God's promise to resurrect me in a new healthy body when His kingdom on Earth was established?

I pointed to the crucifix on the wall and she smiled with that knowing air common to all fanatics and told me that the cross couldn't save my soul and that if I'd just watch the video, I'd understand. She wasn't taking 'No' for an answer and I was ready to drive a stake through her heart. All this while, the patient had been sitting quietly, letting her 'friend' do all the talking. Finally she spoke up and said that maybe I was too busy just now to watch a video and I could look at it later.

I nodded with some relief although the 'friend' looked doubtful. I sent them both to my scheduler to set a date for surgery, then fled to my next patient.

Touch

Surgery is a contact sport. It seems obvious that surgeons touch their patients. We enter their bodies in a way that is both impersonal and incredibly intimate. But beyond the act of operating on someone, touch is a therapeutic tool. I never leave a patient's room or the exam room without touching my patient in a nonclinical way. It may be a handshake, a light touch on the arm, a reassuring squeeze to the top of a foot as I pass the foot of their bed. It has become so internalized that I hardly notice. But the patient does. They tell me that it helps them recognize that they are still a person and not totally consumed by their disease. The longer the patient is ill, the more important the touch becomes.

I always knew I wanted to be a surgeon. From the time I started grade school, it's all I ever wanted to be. It was one thing to want to be something but another to really understand what it meant to reach inside another body. The first time, as a third year medical student that a cardiac surgeon invited me to lay my hand on the beating heart, I fell in love. The feel of the life pumping through the chambers was intoxicating.

Over time, with training, I learned to distinguish the feel of diseased from healthy tissue; the hard scabrous feel of a cancer from the smooth hardness of ordinary scar tissue; the slick softness of the bowel wall from the rubbery softness of the mesentery. I do much of my surgery by feel rather than sight. Even with the laparoscope, I can feel the consistency of tissues through the long instruments, the same way a chef senses the stiffness of the egg whites through the whisk of the doneness of the steak through the tongs. This is a form of healing touch as well, but one that takes place without the patient's direct participation.

The value of the therapeutic touch is being marginalized by the pressures of time and the diffusion of responsibility through the emphasis on team care. No one takes ultimate responsibility for the patient, and although other team members touch the patient, touch without the investment of responsibility carries no sense of caring and no therapy.

Recovery and Hope

I saw a patient in follow up in the office today. She thanked me profusely for saving her life and told me the experience had changed her life. She wasn't a trauma patient and I didn't save her life. To be blunt, I kept her from dying from a complication of my surgical error.

Her hospitalization was a twenty-day siege. It started out as an elective repair of a paraesophageal hiatal hernia. Her stomach was pushed up through her diaphragm alongside her esophagus along with her spleen and part of her transverse colon. It was a massive hernia and it was restricting her breathing and causing her pain whenever she tried to eat.

It was a difficult and complex laparoscopic surgery and I thought it went as well as it could. But somewhere in the dissection, I made a small hole in her esophagus and didn't see it during the surgery. It leaked and 24 hours later she was septic and dying. I rushed her back to the OR and fixed the leak, washed out her chest and abdomen and drained the area, but the die was cast. She started down the spiral of complication begetting complication until she ended up on a ventilator with a tracheostomy, in renal failure and needing multiple medications to maintain her blood pressure.

I spent several nights in the ICU essentially running a continual resuscitation. Several times I expected her to die within the hour.

Slowly things turned around. Her infection cleared, her pressure stabilized, we were able to wean the ventilator. After two weeks, the leak sealed and I could feed her. Ultimately she went to a skilled nursing facility and then home.

I gently deflected her praise. I didn't want to harp on the fact that it was a technical error that caused the trouble in the first place. She insisted that her time in the hospital had renewed her religious faith and she had returned to the Church, which she had left years earlier. She felt that her life was enriched by her experience. I thanked her for her praise and returned her hug a little guiltily.

I see trauma patients all the time who survive life-threatening injuries. I also have general surgery patients who are very sick from their disease process. I'm often impressed with how many of them deal with the experience. Some find renewed religious faith. Others find a renewed focus of their marriage or children or career. Many come away with nothing but pain and bitterness. Their experience is tragic and they see it as a continual burden.

In trauma, a distressingly high number simply return to the risky lifestyle that got them in trouble in the first place – drinking and driving, drugs, riding motorcycles without a helmet, etc. We have a logbook or 'repeat offenders', patients who have been through the trauma bay more than once. Some four or five times.

In situations where the severe illness is a result of a surgical complication, I'm ambivalent about my role. I'm always honest about how the complication happened and what I could have done differently, but I try to keep the focus on getting the patient better, on fixing whatever is wrong. I have a duty to clean up my own mess and am not comfortable accepting any praise for doing so.

My patient left the office happy. I was a bit troubled, but glad she had made a good recovery and had gained something positive from her illness.

## V.O.M.I.T., or Not

Mr. Z was known to me from a previous hernia repair a few years earlier and was now in my office with a CT scan report and a consultation from his Primary Care physician. A few weeks earlier he had complained of a persistent pain in the right lower quadrant of his abdomen. His lab studies were normal, his physical exam was unremarkable and the Primary had ordered a CT scan of the abdomen to try to find out what was causing the pain.

The CT report listed a number of abnormalities, which prompted the referral to me. Mr. Z had several 'indeterminate' densities in his left kidney, a fatty liver, a small amount of low density fluid in his pelvis and a '1.8 cm solid soft tissue mass' in the mesentery of the right lower abdomen. While all of these findings were indeed abnormal, none of them explained his pain, nor were they diagnostic of any significant medical problem. The kidney lesions were most likely cysts. A fatty liver wasn't unusual for a 60+ year-old with type II diabetes. The mesenteric mass was suspicious, but was far too small to cause any symptoms and most likely was a chronically enlarged lymph node. Nevertheless, the radiologist had dutifully reported the findings and had listed a differential diagnosis that included malignancy and had recommended an ultrasound of the kidney and an MRI of the abdomen for further evaluation.

Mr. Z appeared to be a V.O.M.I.T – a Victim Of Medical Imaging Technology. We see this more and more as our ability to image the body improves. Recent news stories have highlighted this problem in routine mammography. Often, breast lesions too small or indistinct to be felt on physical exam are found and require investigation, usually with biopsy. 75% of these biopsies are benign. The remainder are either very early cancers (about 10%) or problems like atypical ductal hyperplasia or lobular carcinoma in situ, entities that are markers for increased risk of breast cancer but which do not need aggressive treatment by themselves. The question of whether a benign biopsy constitutes an "unnecessary" procedure is a debate for another time. The fact remains that the biopsy would not be done without the finding on the imaging study. Sometimes, this process of investigation goes to extremes – a basic image leads to a CT or ultrasound which leads to an MRI or PET scan – imaging study begetting imaging study as each one generates new findings that need explanation.

Perhaps the worst example of this is the incidental finding of small tumors in the adrenal glands. The adrenal glands sit on top of each kidney and produce stress hormones and steroids – epinephrine, cortisol, aldosterone, and ADH (antidiuretic hormone) are all adrenal hormones. Small tumors of the glands are common and most are benign. Cancers of the adrenals do occur, however, as do functional tumors (those that make hormones but do not respond to the normal controls the body exerts to turn hormone production on or off). CT scanning of the abdomen finds these small tumors so often that the have been given the tongue-in-cheek name 'Incidentalomas' when reporting on them. There are protocols for evaluating them. The point is that the finding of one of these triggers another round of imaging and testing to prove that the tumor is benign, all of which does nothing to improve the patient's health or well-being. The incidence of something needing intervention in the evaluation of these incidentalomas is less than 5%. Meanwhile the patient is made anxious and has a number of uncomfortable or expensive tests done. Hence the term V.O.M.I.T..

M. Z had all of the hallmarks of the V.O.M.I.T. syndrome: a study done for a vague unexplained symptom that revealed unsuspected and asymptomatic abnormalities requiring further investigation but that did not explain the original complaint that initiated the investigation.

I examined him and found no physical findings to explain his pain, nor any that indicated the cause of the imaging abnormalities. We sent him off for the MRI as recommended by radiology, even though I doubted it would find anything of surgical significance.

The MRI confirmed that the kidney lesions were complex cysts (benign finding) that required no intervention. It confirmed the fatty liver, again benign if not healthy. The fluid was water density, consistent with minimal ascites (not uncommon in fatty livers). But the mass in the mesentery was read as 'a spiculated enhancing soft tissue mass consistent with infectious adenopathy. Carcinoid tumor metastatic to the area could also have this appearance'.

Thank you, very much. I now had the obligation to prove that this asymptomatic mass, no bigger than a plum pit, wasn't a malignant tumor. Easier said than done. The mesentery is the fan like structure that supports the intestine. All the blood vessels, lymph nodes and veins draining the gut run through it. It is encased in fat and is one of the primary fat stores of the body, far more readily mobilized for energy than the fat under the skin. Finding a small mass in the mesentery is like finding a small rock hidden in a large quilt.

I discussed the approach with Mr. Z, including the option of doing nothing other than repeating the imaging in a few months. In order to remove or biopsy this mass, I would try to find it with a laparoscope. But I would likely need to make an incision large enough to put my hand inside as well - a hand assisted laparoscopy, since only my fingers were likely to be able to feel a 1.8 cm mass in all that fat. He was convinced that the mass had something to do with his pain and insisted that I do something about it.

We went to surgery a week or so later. As expected, at first I saw nothing unusual with the laparoscope. Then I noticed a small segment of intestine that appeared stuck to the mesentery adjacent to it. I made a 6 cm incision, large enough to slip my hand in. (I have small hands and the skin stretches). Sure enough, there was a hard mass in the area, just about the size of the lesion on the MRI. I delivered the small section of bowel through my incision and resected about 4 inches of it. It contained a hard tumor arising from the outer edge of the intestine. Mr. Z recovered well and went home the next day. The pathology report came back as a carcinoid tumor, transmural, with no tumor seen in three adjacent lymph nodes. The surgery probably cured him, although he'll need regular follow up – with MORE imaging studies – for the next few years.

Sometimes even V.O.M.I.T.'s have real disease. He still has pain in his abdomen that I can't explain.

Judgments

About five in the afternoon on a weekday trauma shift we got a call from Native Air, a helicopter medical transport service, about a seventeen year old they were bringing us with multiple fractures sustained in an ATV crash. The accident happened way up in the northern part of the state near St. Johns, a ranching community that borders the Navajo reservation. His vital signs were stable and they had medicated him for pain and would arrive in ten minutes.

The trauma team assembled in the bay closest to the elevator from the helipad. About nine minutes later the elevator doors opened and the helicopter crew wheeled our patient in on their flight gurney.

I took one look at the patient and cursed under my breath. He had a triangular face with a broad forehead and narrow jaw and chin. His chest was wide and deep, barrel-shaped is the term. His limbs were painfully thin with knobby joints and marked curvature of the long bones, those that weren't already splinted. His eyes were striking – deep blue, and the scleras, the white of the eyes, were the color of a new robin's egg. All the markers of Osteogenesis Imperfecta. What the hell was he doing on an ATV?

Osteogenesis Imperfecta, also known as 'brittle bone disease', is a genetic disorder, a gene mutation that causes defective collagen synthesis. It may vary in severity but the classic expression causes weak bones that can break under the patient's own weight. A sneeze can break ribs. A simple stumble can result in a broken hip or ankle. Patients usually end up confined to wheelchairs by their mid-teens, and although they may have a normal lifespan, the repeated fractures lead to short limbs and the characteristic facial appearance. So what monumental stupidity would lead someone who could break a leg just walking on level ground to get on an ATV and ride it around? Then he told me the machine had been a gift from his parents for his birthday, just a couple of weeks earlier.

I almost went ballistic. This wasn't just stupidity, this was child abuse. What kind of parent would willfully place a child with this disease in that kind of danger?

It took a couple of hours to get his x-rays done, get all the fractures identified and splinted, talk to the orthopedic surgeon, and get his pain under at least marginal control. He had fractures of both femurs (the long bone in the thigh), five ribs on the right, the right radius and ulna (the bones of his forearm), and his left ankle. All were fragmented, would need operative repair, and were at high risk for nonunion (failure to heal).

Just as we were getting him ready to go to the OR for the first of many expected procedures, the charge nurse told me his mother was in the waiting area. St. Johns is a long way from our trauma center and she had come by car rather than air. I stalked from the trauma bay, struggling to control my anger.

I found her in the quiet room just off of the main ER. She was in jeans, heavy work boots, and a flannel shirt. Her hair was pulled back and her face was dirty with dark soil and sweat. I introduced myself rather coldly and outlined her son's injuries, the plan for his immediate surgery, and some of the future procedures he would need. She listened calmly but there were unshed tears in her eyes.

"He'll be OK, won't he?" she asked.

"He'll live, but he may not walk and there's a good chance some of those bones won't heal," I said. Then my self-control broke. "How could you let him ride that thing?" I demanded.

Then she did cry. "He was so happy," she said. "Finally he could come down to the corrals and be with us during the day."

She explained that they lived on a ranch three miles from their nearest neighbor. Her son had an all-terrain wheelchair but the path to the corrals where they raised horses was too rough even for that. He had been confined to the house and front yard for several years while the rest of the family worked the ranch. He'd been terribly lonely. They knew the risk when they got him the ATV, but he had begged to be able to come down to the corral and watch her work with the animals.

I was now ashamed of my outburst. I did my best to reassure her that her son was in the best hands and that we would do everything possible to help him. Then I showed her how to get to the preop area so she could see her child.

Surgeons are acutely aware of risk. We make judgments every day about the relative risk versus benefit of our procedures, of the patient's ability to tolerate an operation, of the chance that complications will outweigh potential benefits. Those are calculations that we try to base on our best understanding of physiology, our own abilities and the patient's health. Sometimes we have to accept that the risk of our actions will be high but that the patient has no other option. When the consequences of inaction are not acceptable, we (and our patients) must accept the risk and do our best

There are other risk assessments that people make every day. We take risks when we love someone, when we get married, when we have children. A special risk assessment parents constantly face is the risk of harm to our children versus the need to allow them to learn independence and find their own freedom. What had it cost this mother to make that judgment and come up wrong? I hope I never have to learn that for myself.

## Follow Up

It was a routine Friday night trauma shift and the team was gathering for what sounded like a TINO – Trauma In Name Only; a rollover MVA with a single driver who self extricated and was walking around at the scene slightly confused but with no obvious signs of injury.

I was sitting at the x-ray computer station when the tech came up and said, "Excuse me Doc. I need to log on."

I stood and he caught sight of my face. "Oh! Hi Dr. Davis," he said smiling. "I hoped you'd be on for my first shift. I just started here two weeks ago and this is my first time on nights."

I smiled back, puzzled. He seemed to know me but I couldn't place him. He wasn't one of the regular techs and I didn't remember seeing him at the other hospital where I work. His nametag read 'Larry', but that didn't ring any bells.

He nodded and said, "I didn't think you'd recognize me. Ten years ago, when I was sixteen you operated on me and took out half my liver."

It came back to me then. He was a good foot taller and at least thirty pounds heavier, but now that he'd reminded me I knew him.

That night, ten years earlier, he'd been brought in after being hit by a car while skateboarding. He was in shock and going downhill fast.

We loaded him with volume, packed red blood cells, saline and later, plasma. This was before the institution of the massive transfusion protocol with its balance of red cells and plasma and automatic sending of components at timed intervals. We struggled to keep up with his falling vitals. His abdomen was getting distended and rather than risk him crashing in CT, I did a diagnostic peritoneal lavage. A catheter is inserted into the abdomen through a small incision in the umbilicus (belly button) and if you get blood back, it's a sign of internal bleeding. Not a refined test, and these days, antiquated by the FAST ultrasound scan and the rapid acquisition CT, but back then it was often done if the patient was unstable. Blood bubbled up from my small incision before I could even insert the catheter.

We rushed off to the OR and explored his abdomen. He had cracked his liver through the central sinus, just behind the gallbladder.

Your liver looks like a homogeneous organ, but in fact is divided into right and left lobes by a band of tissue and a central vein just behind the gallbladder. Further segmental divisions are based on the branching of the portal and hepatic veins and although they are real, they are not as well defined. This boy's liver was smashed. Most of the right lobe was hamburger and the large fracture through the central sinus was bleeding at an alarming rate.

I tried to suture individual vessels, to clip large bleeders and control the bile ducts, but he continued to bleed from almost every surface. Finally, 15 units of packed cells into the procedure, I packed the wound in the liver with bulky gauze pads, compressed the smashed tissue between several other gauze packs and closed the abdomen with the packs inside.

It's called Damage Control Surgery. The concept is based on the Navy doctrine of Damage Control on combat ships. When a warship is damaged in action, it can't retire to a nearby shipyard for repairs. The crew must patch the leaks and holes with anything at hand and jury rig systems to function well enough to continue the fight or sail away to safety. So too, when you get behind the physiologic curve in the OR, you need to patch the leaks quickly, staple off or tie off holes in bowel or bladder and bail out with a plan to return another day for definitive repairs once the patient is stable.

I managed to control the bleeding with the packs and we moved him to the ICU. He got more fluid, blood components and most importantly he got warm. Heat loss in the OR is a major contributing factor to bleeding. By warming him up, replacing the losses and stabilizing his vitals, he lived to fight another day. 48 hours later, I took him back to surgery and removed the packs, controlled what was now minimal bleeding and removed much of the right lobe of his liver. There was very little new bleeding. He recovered over the next three weeks and left the hospital.

Flash forward ten years and here he is standing in front of me, twenty-six years old, and six and a half feet tall and obviously in the prime of his young life. He told me he had recovered fast enough that he stayed in his regular high school class and graduated on time. He learned to be an x-ray tech during a five-year tour in the Army after high school and had just moved back to Arizona with his wife and two daughters, aged two and three.

He still works trauma and general x-ray and we see each other frequently. It's not often that I get to see the long-term results of what we do in the trauma bay, but this one is special to me. Larry is a good tech, a nice guy, and when his daughters have come to see him on the job, he looks like a good Dad. Seeing him banishes many of the feelings of futility that I have from time to time.

Teamwork

Trauma is a team sport. Surgeons are not, by nature, team players. Too much emphasis on individual responsibility in training, perhaps. Or perhaps surgical training appeals to a particular type of hyper-responsible person. The nature of trauma demands an ability to put aside the need to be the Lone Ranger and know when to call for help. It's a lesson that took me many years to learn.

Last Friday EMS brought us a patient with multiple gunshot wounds. He had been shot in the back just to the right of the midline at the level of the second lumbar vertebra, about a hand's breadth below the ribcage. He had a second wound in the left thigh that went through and through in a zone that has little in the way of critical structures and a third wound that shattered the lower right leg with a large area of tissue loss. His vital signs were relatively stable but he could not move his legs and had no sensation below the level of the pelvic brim.

We took a quick chest and abdominal x-ray to see where the bullet in his back had gone. His second lumbar vertebra was shattered and his loss of function and sensation suggested a spinal cord injury. The bullet was in the muscles of the anterior abdominal wall, having entered posteriorly.

Transabdominal gunshot wounds are never (or almost never) benign. The zone where the bullet had passed in this man was full of traps for the unwary surgeon. One could make the case for going straight to the operating room with a wound such as this. Wherever the bullet had gone it had almost certainly hit something deadly on its path. I opted to do a CT scan first. In part because I wanted a look at his kidneys and in art because I wanted to see his aorta. Both were potentially in the path of this wound.

The bullet track was visible on CT as a trail of air bubble, bone fragments and metallic debris. The aorta was intact but the vena cava was compressed. The bullet passed between these two big vessels, then through the left lobe of the liver. Somehow it appeared to have missed the pancreas and the right kidney.

I took him to surgery intending to look for any sign of bowel injury, assess the liver and try to stay away from the aorta or cava, since there didn't seem to be active bleeding.

It was mid afternoon, so I had extra nurses and techs to help set up and a scrub tech to assist me. We opened the abdomen and removed some bullet fragments and clot. There was a large collection of blood around the duodenum, the first part of the small intestine, and I was worried about a possible perforation of the bowel there. I gently tried to mobilize that segment and immediately knew I was in trouble. Opening the tissue plane around the duodenum released the clot that had formed around the vena cava. The abdomen filled up with blood as if someone had turned on a tap full blast.

I told the anesthesiologist we had major bleeding and then stuck my fingers in the hole from which the blood gushed fast enough to be audible, like water running in a sink. I could feel but not see the edge of the cava. The bullet had clipped off a 2 cm long chunk of the side wall of the vessel. I couldn't mobilize it and repair it because every time I moved my finger the blood filled the field. I could control the bleeding with pressure, but then only had one hand to try to get control of the blood vessel. The surgical tech was good but this was out of her league.

After a couple of futile attempts which resulted in more bleeding and the anesthesiologist cursing at me for dropping the blood pressure to almost nothing, I turned to the room nurse and said, "See if Dr. V. is still in house and ask him to come in here."

We spent the few minutes it took for my colleague to come down from the ICU holding pressure on the hole and pumping in blood and factors.

Dr. V stuck his head in and asked, "What have you got?"

"A hole in the cava just above the head of the pancreas. Side wall at least and maybe the back wall, too."

"I'll scrub." was all he said.

I didn't have to ask for help. It was understood when I called him into the room and described the injury. My scrub tech that day was good, but I needed some more active and experienced help. I needed someone who had faced this himself and knew what I needed to see when I needed to see it and didn't need to be told.

With Dr. V.'s help exposing the vessel, I was able to define the larger of the two holes and sew it closed. The patient was still bleeding from the smaller hole in the back wall, but I was able to rotate the vessel enough so that Dr. V could see it and put a stitch in.

Meanwhile, the anesthesiologist had been running the massive transfusion protocol. Under that plan, the blood bank sent a cooler of packed red blood cells, plasma, platelets and clotting factors every fifteen minutes until we hollered stop. She had kept up with bleeding that literally made a noise when I wasn't compressing the cava and the patient now had a normal blood pressure. Teamwork.

Dr. V excused himself now that the bleeding was controlled. I cleaned up some minor bleeding in the field, closed the holes in the liver and closed the abdomen.

We next called the neurosurgeon who came in and put stabilizing rods in the spine bridging the shattered vertebra and keeping it from shifting. Then the orthopedic surgeon came and cleaned up the leg and splinted it. We moved the patient to the ICU where he remained stable for the rest of the night.

The point of this story isn't the save itself, although that felt pretty good. The point is that it was a team effort. Dr. V and I, the anesthesiologist, the tech and the nurse, even the neurosurgeon and the orthopod all played major roles in getting the patient through the surgery. I could not have done the surgery alone, although there was a time in my career when I would have tried. Without the stellar work by anesthesia, the patient would have bled out before we could get control of the cava. Without the neurosurgeon, the unstable spine fracture may have shifted doing more damage to the area. Without the orthopedic surgeon, the open fracture would have become infected and the patient might have died despite our efforts.

Putting together a team that works well together is hard. There needs to be an atmosphere of trust in each other's abilities and a certain amount of familiarity to be able to function smoothly in a crisis. Sometimes it works better than others, depending on the relative skills of the team members and on intangibles such as personality and shared experience.

I was fortunate to have people around me that I knew and trusted on this case. I could let them do their jobs and trust that they would do the right thing. Sometimes, administrators fail to recognize the value of teamwork. To many of them we are interchangeable widgets; one is as good as another. Contracts are let based on low bids rather than on experience and integrity. So far, that hasn't been a problem at my trauma center, but I fear the day is coming when I will bring a critically ill patient to the OR and face a temporary contact anesthesiologist I have never met and who is only working that day, never to be seen again.

## 100 Years Old

Tomorrow I will operate on a 100-year-old patient. She is frail and a bit forgetful but knows her family and understands her disease and the proposed surgery. She's a bit hard of hearing but is otherwise healthy for her age. And she has cancer. She's not suffering from it now; it isn't causing her any pain even though the tumor is quite large. In a few months it will become a significant problem. So she, her primary care doctor, her family, and I all agree that she should have surgery to remove the tumor. By any standard she is a high-risk patient, but hopefully the risk is acceptable in order to prevent a great deal of misery later. I'm not implying that the surgery isn't needed, (although in a future world where Prospective Payment Committees decide what Medicare will pay for, this surgery might not be covered) or that this situation is unusual. Quite the opposite. Although this woman's age is at the upper end of my patient population, I routinely do complex surgery on octogenarians. My hernia patient on Monday was 92. The average age on the trauma census is often over 70. The population I see is skewed somewhat by Arizona being a popular retirement destination, but the trend is clear. My baby-boomer cohorts and I are getting older. The system is ill prepared to care for us.

Jim

Emergency room call is always a pain. By and large you are presented with sick people who really don't want to be there. By definition, emergencies are unexpected and when people find themselves in the ER with an acute surgical problem (other than a trauma) it's always at a bad time for them. Sometimes part of your job is to convince them that they really are sick and really, really need surgery.

Jim was one of those patients. He came to the ER because his wife had gotten tired of him griping about his stomachache over the past three days. When he got weak and dizzy getting out of a chair, he finally listened to her and they drove to the Emergency Room.

The ER docs worked him up with the usual CT scan of the abdomen, the default test these days for abdominal pain (see my post on Abominable Pain on the website for my feelings on this betrayal of diagnostic medicine). Then they called me.

Jim had severe pancreatitis as well as a distended and thickened gallbladder that was packed with stones. The CT showed fluid and gas around his pancreas, free fluid in his abdomen and thickening of the root of his small bowel mesentery (the structure that contains all the blood vessels to the small bowel). These are all grave signs of a severe form of pancreatitis called necrotizing pancreatitis.

He was a basically healthy, if moderately obese, 54 year-old guy; a retired Marine who thought he could tough out 'a little indigestion'. Oh, and his daughter was an ultrasound tech who worked at my primary hospital and had requested me, (another grave sign. Families of healthcare workers always seem to do poorly).

Pancreatitis is a common but poorly understood disease. Poorly understood in that we're not sure exactly why it starts. The disease process is straight forward enough – all the digestive enzymes that usually are secreted into the intestine and attack the foods we eat, breaking them down into component sugars and amino acids that we can absorb, start to attack the pancreas itself, essentially autodigesting it. This leads to pain and inflammation, tissue death, and sometimes infection. Imagine pouring acid into your abdomen and you get the idea. Forty percent of cases of pancreatitis are caused by gallbladder disease. We think stones or bile crystals escape from the gallbladder and travel down the bile duct, which passes through the pancreas. Along the way, it is thought, they damage the lining of the common channel the bile duct and pancreatic duct share, allowing the enzymes to seep into the surrounding tissue. The resulting damage causes more leakage and so it starts.

Most pancreatitis is mild to moderate causing abdominal pain and some fluid shifts that are easily treated with pain medications and IV fluids. Occasionally, though, the damage is fulminant and rapidly progresses to necrosis (tissue death) of the pancreas. This is the equivalent of a third degree burn inside the abdomen. Bacteria love dead tissue and pancreatic infection, abscesses, and generalized sepsis and circulatory collapse can quickly follow. The process affects multiple systems from the lungs to the kidneys and often ends in multiple organ system failure and death.

Jim was teetering on the edge of disaster, although he didn't know it yet. Surgery for pancreatitis is limited to draining fluid collections and debriding, or cutting away, infected tissue. It's often a matter of delicate timing. Operate too soon and you worsen the necrosis by irritating the inflamed tissue, or you stir up dangerous bleeding from the rich network of small blood vessels that feed the pancreas. Too late and your patient is too sick for a definitive operation and you end up doing less than enough to halt the process.

The first priority in Jim's situation was to resuscitate him with fluids. He was leaking internally, enough that he was profoundly dehydrated. The second was convincing him he needed to stay in the hospital. The third was to get his gallbladder out. This was necessary to stop further damage and to treat what had now become an acute infection.

He refused at first, but after a pointed conversation with his wife, agreed to stay, just for the night. I started writing some orders to get him admitted and called the OR to check on room availability. Just as I hung up, the nurse pushed the code button. Jim's blood pressure had dropped too low to be recordable and he was unconscious. We pushed several liter of fluid into him, started drugs to support his blood pressure, and rushed off to surgery.

When I opened his abdomen, a rush of gray, foul smelling fluid greeted me. His gallbladder was dead – a sickly greenish-black color – and the pancreas was the color of rotten meat. I took out the gallbladder quickly and elevated his stomach to expose the pancreas. It was the consistency of cottage cheese and I scooped the dead and dying tissue out until I encountered something that bled. I packed the abdomen and left it open with a vacuum dressing in place.

By this point, Jim was barely alive. Supported by a ventilator and three different pressors - drugs to elevate his blood pressure – we moved him to the ICU.

We took him back to surgery six times over the next two weeks, changing the packs, debriding more dead tissue and eventually closing his abdomen. His kidneys shut down for a while; he needed the ventilator to support his breathing for the entire time and required a tracheostomy; he developed one infection after another and eventually ended up of three antibiotics and an antifungal. His colon perforated and leaked after the enzymes eroded a hole in it and he needed a colostomy; his wound broke down and needed to be reclosed; he bled from an artery next to the pancreas and fortunately the radiologist was able to embolize it because I'd have killed him with another operation at that point. For a while it was one complication after another to the point where I dreaded making rounds for fear that some new crisis would declare itself.

Slowly things turned around and he began the long road to recovery. He spent a total of three months in the hospital and another six weeks in rehab.

Finally, four months to the day from our first meeting in the ER, he returned to the office for a follow up and to remove his tracheostomy tube.

The first words he said after I removed the tube and he could speak again were, "So, Doc, did I really need to stay in the hospital, or could I have toughed it out at home?"

I didn't know how to answer that without making him sound stupid. His wife looked ready to smack him and started to apologize to me. Then I saw the grin on his face.

"Gotcha," he said. Then he shook my hand. "Semper Fi, Doc. They told me you'd been in the Corps so I knew you weren't BS'ing me."

"Semper Fi, Gunny," was all I could say.

J. D.

It was early on a Monday evening and I had been home for about an hour when my phone rang. I answered and my friend and colleague, Dr. Nick S. was on the line.

"J.D. is here in the ER again," he said. "Do you want me to write some holding orders for him?"

"How bad is it this time?" I asked.

"Worse than last week," Nick said. "He's in a lot of pain and has been vomiting since yesterday morning. He's pretty dehydrated right now. I'm giving him a liter of saline but he'll need to come in."

"I'll come. Give me a half hour or so," I said.

J.D. was a long time patient of mine. He showed up in the ER every few days with signs of a bowel obstruction. I'd admit him and pretend to treat him. He'd tell me jokes and pretend to get better. J.D. had widely metastatic carcinoid. His abdomen was full of tumor and there wasn't anything surgical I could do for him.

Up until his 69th birthday, he'd been a healthy, almost obsessively fit athlete. He competed in senior triathlons, had the resting heart rate of a twenty-year-old, took no medications other than vitamins, and ran 5 miles before breakfast every other day. He complained to his Primary Care about a pain in his right lower abdomen. The Primary felt a vague mass and ordered a CT scan. The scan showed a massively enlarged appendix and he was sent to me.

I operated on him a few days later. There was a hard mass at the base of his appendix that obstructed the outlet and caused it to back up and enlarge. The mass proved to be a carcinoid tumor on frozen section. I resected his right colon, 34 lymph nodes, and found two small masses in the right lobe of his liver. I took them out as well and they proved to be metastases from the tumor in the appendix.

Carcinoid is a malignant tumor of the neuroendocrine cells of the intestine. Unlike more common adenocarcinoma, carcinoid tumors don't start in the lining of the intestine but in the small clusters of hormone secreting cells adjacent to the bowel wall. They are very slow growing, often taking years to spread beyond the original site. Sometimes they are also overactive in secreting the hormone serotonin. If the tumor load is high enough this can lead to the carcinoid syndrome – a complex of flushing, diarrhea, wheezing and edema. It can also damage the heart valves.

There aren't many therapies for carcinoid other then surgical resection. Chemotherapy is ineffective; drugs like somatostatin can limit or control the carcinoid syndrome by inhibiting serotonin, but don't slow the tumor growth.

J.D. did well for the first year after his surgery. He resumed running and competed in the senior division of the Kona ironman triathlon. Then about 13 months after his first operation he came in with a bowel obstruction. It didn't resolve and I took him back to the operating room. There was a recurrent carcinoid narrowing a loop of small bowel. I was able to remove it but knew there would be more trouble down the road. There were dozens of tumor deposits, rice grain tiny, scattered all across the bowel. They were too numerous to remove and too small to be seen on imaging.

Over the next two years J.D.'s carcinoid symptoms got worse. Ultimately he developed another obstruction. After five days, I reluctantly reoperated. This time his abdomen looked like someone had poured concrete into it. I managed to bypass the blockage but also about half of his functional small bowel. He had a difficult recovery and began to lose weight. Over the next six months, I admitted him every couple of weeks for rehydration or pain control. Through it all he remained unfailingly cheerful. There were times when he was at his worst with nausea, diarrhea and pain that he would tell a joke to cheer ME up.

It only took me twenty minutes to get to the ER. I greeted Nick who pointed to the ER bay where J.D. lay. He was down to less than half the weight he'd been when I first met him. His breathing was ragged and his lips were dry and cracked. He smiled at me but didn't speak.

I turned to Carole, J.D.'s wife of forty-three years. "How long has he been like this?" I asked.

"Since yesterday afternoon. He didn't want to come in, but we ran out of the liquid morphine," she said. "He didn't want them to bother you, but I didn't know what else to do."

"It's OK," I said to both of them. "We'll get some fluids and narcotics on board and things will look better in the morning."

I left the bedside to write orders. Carole followed me.

"He's not coming home this time, is he?" she said.

I shook my head. "I don't think so. Hopefully, I can get him more comfortable. I'll talk to him in the morning and see what he wants to do. Did you call the Hospice people after the last time?"

She shook her head. "He didn't want them. He just wants family around when the time comes."

"What about you? Don't you need some help?"

She shook her head. "I'll be fine." She gave me a long hug and whispered, "Thank you." Then she went back to her husband.

By morning J.D was more alert but still very weak. He grinned at me from his hospital bed. "I hear you've been putting the moves on my wife," he whispered. "You could at least wait until I check out."

"I'm married to a Sicilian, J.D.," I said. "If she even thinks I've been fooling around with another woman, I'll be singing soprano."

We laughed and I went to write his discharge order. He insisted on going home again. I had spent an hour the night before trying to convince him to stay, or go into inpatient hospice. He insisted on going home and Carole backed him. I worried about them, about Carole's ability to handle him alone, but they were determined.

It was the last time I saw J.D. alive. Carole called the office two days later and told me that he had died in his sleep. Once again she thanked me for taking care of him.

I told her she was welcome and hung up before I broke down in tears.

All patient deaths affect you but some are harder than others. I had treated J.D. for over five years, had watched the slow, inexorable progression of his disease and felt the helplessness of being unable to cure him. He faced it all with courage and good humor and epitomized the ideal of grace in the face of death.

A few years later, Carole came to my office with her new husband. He had been a family friend when J.D. was alive and his first wife had died a couple of years before J.D. He and Carole had bonded over their shared loss and had married six months before they came to my office. He thought he had a hernia and I was the only surgeon Carole would consider. It turned out to be a pulled muscle rather than a hernia. They were both relieved and pleased. It did me good to see them so happy together. I think J.D would have wanted that, too.

## CARMUDGEONLY OBSERVATIONS

The Devaluing of Experience

One overlooked provision in the New World Order of Healthcare Reform is the change in how consultations by specialists are coded and paid for.

As of 2012, the increased rate of payment for a specialist's evaluation under Medicare is eliminated. We are paid at the same rate as the Primary Care physician for our evaluation and opinion. We can bill for a 'comprehensive exam' if we document that we not only looked at the patient's surgical problem but also determined when they had the chicken pox as a child and what their great aunt Hattie died from.

Never mind that the primary care doctor has already done that and the patient was referred to me for my expert opinion about his gallbladder. Never mind that if the primary care doctor thought he was qualified to take it out, he would have. My years of extra training and experience in the field are of no additional value. If I do a focused exam on the surgical problem and the relevant comorbidities, I get less than the nurse practitioner who does the three-page history and physical exam.

Now this may seem like a petty complaint. After all, why should I get more for an evaluation that take me less that fifteen minutes? For the same reason that you expect to pay more for a master carpenter than a construction laborer. Or for an original work of art rather than a print. There is an old saying that surgical training is six years long because it takes two years to teach you how to operate and four more to teach you when not to operate.

Judgment and experience have real value in this profession, but not according to the government bureaucrats who write the rules. To them, we are all equal, right tsovaritch?

An Ethical Dilemma

Cicero once said, "Treat not with men who have no honor. You are both dishonored in the exchange but they have nothing to lose."

What then is the proper course of action when confronted with a powerful organization that one believes is behaving unethically? The easy answer, the one that most people will give automatically (and somewhat self-righteously), is to refuse to do business with that organization.

But what if the organization is behaving in a perfectly legal and businesslike manner? What if, nevertheless, that behavior violates you own code of ethics, and arguably the larger ethical standard of 'what is right and just'?

I find myself wrestling with that question right now. Many of my peers think I'm overstating the problem or that I'm being too idealistic. Many agree that the organization may not be a paragon of virtue, but they are scrupulously obeying the letter of the law, so there are no grounds for complaint.

The large hospital system that operates the hospital where I do most of my elective surgery (not the trauma center where I also work) has instituted a policy of requiring payment in full of that portion of the total bill for which the patient is responsible BEFORE any non-emergent surgery can be scheduled. In other words, if you have one of the 80/20 insurance plans sold under the ACA exchange, or if your employer provided plan has such a payment scheme, the hospital wants your 20% up front. They won't waive it or let you finance it other than on a major credit card. The only exceptions are 'emergencies'.

So far so good. I don't have a big problem with such a policy for purely elective surgery such as the asymptomatic hernia or the elective hysterectomy or gallbladder surgery. But the hospital is taking a hard line on what constitutes and emergency. Specifically, an emergency is a life or limb threatening problem or one that will cause the patient irreparable harm if not treated immediately. The key word is immediately, as in today, not tomorrow or next week.

Recently I received word from yet another patient that she was unable to go ahead with surgery due to the policy of demanding payment in advance of her copayment of 20% of her anticipated hospital bill. I was asked if her surgery was an emergency. Usually for scheduled cases I do not certify them as emergent, but in this case I answered that it was. The patient had originally been scheduled for a laparoscopic cholecystectomy in August, but came to my office urgently this week with crescendo symptoms. Her right upper quadrant pain had become much worse and was now almost continuous and required narcotics for control. I moved her surgery up to July 9, 48 hours after seeing her in my office. She went straight to the registration area to set up her surgery and was told she would have to pay a large sum in advance based on her insurance plan. She did not have the money or the available credit on a credit card to pay. After I said it was an emergency, she was referred to hospitals Chief Medical Officer who reviewed her case and apparently her finances and somehow decided that it was appropriate for her to pay $500. Again, she stated she did not have that much cash and so she cancelled her surgery. I eventually did her surgery at the trauma center where I work and where there is no review of a surgeon's decision that a surgery is urgent or emergent. This is not the first time this has occurred. I and several other surgeons have had patients in need of cancer surgery have the same issue with respect to demands for advance payment of large sums prior to scheduling surgery. I have discussed this personally with the CMO and also with the Medical Staff President. While I understand the issue of bad debt resulting from patients failing to pay their share of their medical bills, I have little sympathy for the system's pleas of financial hardship as a result of it. On any given day, thirty to forty percent of my billing is bad debt. As a solo private practitioner, my ability to tolerate and finance that debt is surely more limited than a large organization such as the one that owns and operates my primary hospital. If this bad debt is so crippling, then how is this same hospital system able to buy hospitals all over the state and take over management of the U of A medical school? I object strongly to having my clinical judgment as a surgeon over ruled by the hospital CMO, especially when he is neither a surgeon nor in the active day-to-day practice of patient care. I further think it is inappropriate for him to be making financial judgments with respect to a patient's ability to pay. It is one thing to ask for advance payment for a purely elective surgery such as the repair of an asymptomatic hernia. It is both medically and morally indefensible to place financial considerations ahead of care in cases of cancer surgery or where a surgeon has declared that the surgery is urgent or emergent. To limit waiver of the advance payment to life threatening emergencies only may satisfy any legal responsibility, but such a policy compromises patient care in situation such as my patient's. She did not have a life-threatening problem but was unable to function normally until her surgical disease was addressed. This policy needs to be changed. I know the satisfaction of a single patient means little to the hospital, but this particular patient has refused to have anything to do with the hospital, now or in the future. As more and more people experience similar treatment, patient satisfaction is sure to suffer.

I suggest that first, the CMO actually discuss the clinical situation with the patient's surgeon if he chooses to over rule the declaration of an emergency. Second, a third category of 'urgent but not emergent' needs to be created for patients such as mine – people who are not in imminent danger of death or complication but who still need surgery as soon as practically possible. Third, the CMO should be removed from any financial decision making about how much it is appropriate for a patient to pay if that is to be less than full payment. There are financial professionals who do that job all the time in the business world. The hospital needs to hire appropriate people to look at this issue the same way that a debt counseling service would. The current situation is unconscionable for an organization that professes to make a positive difference in people's lives.

While the policy is unquestionably legal, adhering to the strict letter of the law, it is not, in my opinion, ethical. It does not support justice or do what is best for the patients who seek care at this institution.

So what does a lone surgeon do? I have written multiple letters of protest, brought the subject up at departmental meetings, and had conversations with the CMO and the CEO of the hospital, all of which have proven futile. Do I continue to bring my patients here and thereby tacitly support this policy? Do I resign from the staff? That would hurt no one but me. In fact, I'm sure the CEO and a number of administrators would be glad to have me out of their hair. Resigning would also inconvenience my patients, most of whom live near my office. There is no alternative hospital that isn't owned by the same system within 15 miles.

For now, I will continue to protest this policy at every opportunity. But am I just being naïve? Is this the way of the future? The ACA has made the high deductible, 80/20 plans the industry standard. There will be more pressure on hospitals and patients both. But through all the argument over personal responsibility, bad debt, and the definitions of medical necessity and emergency care, we need to maintain or commitment to doing what is best for our patients. We need to continue to do right and seek justice.

Abominable Pain

A few months ago one of those silly Facebook surveys asked me to name the ten most influential books in my life. One of the ten was a slim volume by Sir Zachary Cope entitled 'Early Diagnosis of the Acute Abdomen'. It is the surgeon's Bible when it comes to examining the abdomen. With a clear understanding of the principles outlined in the book, an astute surgeon can evaluate a patient in a few minutes and come to a diagnosis of the cause of the patient's abdominal pain with a 70 to 85% confidence level. Further testing can then refine that to near 100%.

A few simple questions about the patient's pain are the key. When did it start? Was the onset sudden or gradual? Where is it located? Does it move? What is the nature of the pain? Burning? Sharp or stabbing? Dull or aching? Cramping? What makes the pain worse or better? Associated symptoms like nausea, vomiting, diarrhea, fever, sweating?

Simple lab and x-ray tests add more information- a Complete Blood Count, Liver function assay, and enzyme tests for pancreatic enzymes plus a plain upright abdominal x-ray may be all that are needed.

Armed with this basic information, an experienced surgeon can diagnose the cause of the pain 90 to 95% of the time. Fancier, more expensive studies such as CT scans, ultrasound, and the like may occasionally be needed to nail down a diagnosis, but should not be the first tests ordered.

I think I'm going to buy a hundred copies of the little book and distribute them to emergency rooms all over my city. The current diagnostic test of choice for abdominal pain, any abdominal pain, seems to be a CT with contrast. I understand the reason. The doctor gets immediate feedback without the need to think very hard and the patient gets the reassurance of a high tech test. That doesn't make it right. There are cost issues and, although I tend to pooh-pooh it, issues of radiation exposure. And there's the bigger issue of professionalism.

Maybe I'm too curmudgeonly, or just a dinosaur, but since when was an x-ray a substitute for a careful history and physical exam? I am often called to see a patient for abdominal pain and an "abnormal CT' only to find clear evidence that no one has even looked at the abdomen. I would not have the temerity to compare myself to Ochsner or Halsted or Gross, the gurus of physical diagnosis from the beginning of the last century, but I am dismayed at how far we have strayed from their teachings. Some of my younger colleagues would have a hard time finding their ass with both hands without a CT scan. And whatever the radiologist reports on his reading of the scan is taken as Gospel, even if only mentioned as part of a differential diagnosis and a simple assessment of the physical findings would rule it out.

What is lacking, and getting harder to find, is the direct bedside evaluation of the physical signs and symptoms, the hands-on exam, and the gestalt assessment that comes from experience. Experience comes from doing the exam over and over and correlating it with the findings at surgery. But if you don't do the exam in the first place and count on technology to do the work for you, you don't learn.

## The Trouble With Freedom

In my heart, I am a libertarian. I believe in individual freedom and individual responsibility. I believe in limited government--severely limited government. I am not a fan of either political party in this country, but can think of no other place on earth that combines both the protection of individual rights and political stability that this country offers.

That said, I am tired of the exercise of freedom being a license for stupidity. Yes, you are free to drink yourself into oblivion every weekend. But don't get behind the wheel of a car or a powerboat when you do so. Don't decide you are superman and can leap from a roof or a cliff into shallow water. Don't get drunk with people you don't really like and decide to tell them off, especially if they're bigger and more sober than you. I know this is a useless appeal because you are too stupid to understand the consequences of your actions, but I'm the guy who gets to patch you up after your adventure and am tired of hearing the same lame story time after time.

Yes, you should be free to ride your motorcycle without a helmet. After all, freedom is what motorcycles are all about and that sense of free flying with the wind in your hair is part of it. I know my appeal to stop a moment and think about what happens when an unprotected head meets concrete even at low speed has no effect on you, but again I make it. In my more cynical moments, I can support your decision if you'd guarantee that you'd become an organ donor. At least then someone would benefit from your stupidity.

You are free to supersize your meals, buy all that wonderfully convenient fast food. I'm a big fan of Whataburger myself. If you are unable to exercise restraint and self control you can always blame it on McDonalds. And when your diabetes and hypertension and heart disease leave you unable to do more than sit on the couch and watch reality TV, you can always go on disability. Healthcare is a right, right? So no matter what you do to yourself, someone else is obligated to pay for taking care of you.

Shouldn't we pass laws requiring motorcycle helmets? Shouldn't we pass laws that forbid drinking and driving or operating machinery? Shouldn't we forbid motorcycles entirely as unsafe at any speed? Shouldn't we outlaw cigarettes and high fat fast foods and sugar-laden sodas? Ah, there's the rub. Where do we draw the line? 'Reasonable people' agree with drunk driving laws and motorcycle helmet laws and minimum drinking age laws. But 'reasonable people' can also be persuaded to ban particular foods or drugs or activities as too risky. The world is full of zealous people of infinite good will who will try to convince me that an organic bran muffin and herbal tea are just as satisfying as a Moon Pie and an RC Cola.

I know that personal freedom isn't an all or nothing absolute. And I see daily the consequences of stupidity in the exercise of freedom, at least as far as trauma and personal health are concerned.

One of the arguments for universal health care is the cost of caring for uninsured patient who get sick from preventable illness. I don't really agree with the position, since there is evidence that preventive care doesn't reduce costs. It improves quality of life and delays catastrophic complications, but the actual cost of care is higher. That's an argument for another time.

My point is that to affect chronic stupidity, you need to pass laws that intervene directly in people's personal lives and choices. Helmet laws and drunk driving laws are reasonable and prudent, but what about smoking bans? What about limits on the fat content in foods? What about government monitoring of a child's Body Mass Index in the school? What about required end of life discussions with elderly patients? When do 'reasonable people' decide what you can and can't eat in the name of protecting your good health?

The problem with freedom is that it includes the freedom to be stupid. Yes, society ends up bearing the costs of stupidity. But there's no cure except the restriction of freedom, a step that requires more forethought and nuance that I'm willing to trust to any government.

Suicide Ain't Painless

Some of the best advice I ever received as a medical student was from my chief resident when I was an eager young fourth-year on my first trauma rotation. "Never run to a gunshot wound to the head," he said. "They'll either survive until you get there or they won't survive no matter how fast you run." The corollary to that axiom is "Think donor. The life you save may not be the one in the trauma bay".

Gunshot wounds to the head are a particularly difficult type of trauma to deal with. When self inflicted, they automatically create a lot of ambivalence for the trauma team. It's hard to work to save a life that the patient himself didn't think was worth living. And shooting yourself in the head, unlike taking pills or cutting your wrists, is a statement of a fairly serious intent to end your life.

Mostly it is an act of despair, although sometimes it seems understandable. Not a choice I would make, but understandable for the patient. I am not a psychiatrist for a reason--I have little patience with neurotics and depressed people whose only purpose in life seems to be inflicting their own misery on everyone else around them. So depression, despair, loneliness, all the usual reasons people cite as the cause of their suicidal motivation don't strike me as particularly valid reasons to put a gun to your head. In those cases, it's an act of supreme selfishness.

On the other hand, a patient faced with a long and debilitating and ultimately fatal illness may see suicide as a rational act to avoid a futile and costly struggle that will have the same outcome in the end as a bullet in the brain. Again, not necessarily my choice, but understandable. I'm a firm believer in property rights. The ultimate property right is the right to decide what to do with your own life. If suicide seems a rational decision, I support your right to make that choice. Just get it right the first time and make sure no one else is hurt in the process.

That last part is the real problem with suicide. It may seem right to you, but even the most rational suicide harms those whom you leave behind. Death and grief go hand in hand, but sudden death leaves little time for the survivors to prepare or accept the loss. The thought that you would deliberately choose death over staying with people who care about you is doubly hard for the survivors to accept.

It's a very personal type of rejection and all the rational arguments about why you did it don't change that.

As a trauma surgeon, I give families bad news on a regular basis. It isn't something that I'm particularly good at. Although I try to put things in terms that are easily understood and give an honest assessment of the patient's prognosis, I'm not good at offering comforting words or expressions of sympathy. Harder still is the discussion of brain death and organ donation. I believe in donation. I encourage everyone to become an organ donor. But I'm lousy at broaching the subject with families, even though it's supposed to be part of my job. Thank God for the nurses at Donor Network who do that sort of thing very well.

Change and the Surgical Dinosaur

Dinosaur is a label I wear proudly. I still believe that my patients are my responsibility 24/7. I believe that a daily note in the medical record should be concise, accurate and based on the latest evaluation of the patient, best done within minutes of leaving the bedside. I believe that the cumulative record should be written in such a way that if I should die, another surgeon could review the record and take over care without missing a beat. Simple parameters, almost axiomatic for any medical record.

So what's wrong with going from pen and paper to an all-electronic record? In principal, nothing. In practice, well, the devil is in the details. Let me say up front that I am not a Luddite. I'm not as tech savvy as my son, but I'm pretty comfortable with computers. I use one a lot for writing, posting to a web site, gaming and the like. I'm comfortable with word processing, basic web design, etc. I can do these things because the programs I use have good basic interfaces, intuitive navigation and easy validation and sharing with other programs.

The system chosen by my main hospital for an all-electronic record exemplifies none of those things. While very complete, the interface is complex and counterintuitive. Order entry is fragmented and even with the construction of 'favorites' folders, time consuming. Unless you type a custom note daily, the pre-formatted note templates are choppy and look like a computer-generated checklist. And just for fun, the system can't talk to anything else. The lab, radiology and ER systems are all separate and need complex translation programming to make them work. To view an image, I have to literally log out of the chart and log into a different radiology interface.

Change is inevitable, but change that one doesn't choose and control is disruptive at best, chaotic at worst. Admittedly, surgeons are control freaks. Most of us are convinced that bad things happen when we are not in control. So I try to temper my distrust of this system with the admission that I don't like change even when it is good for me. But I dread the day that the system crashes, or we have a power failure and have nothing to back us up but the assurance of the IT people that they have a plan. I'll hang on to my pen for the time being, thank you.

Protocols Mean No One Has to Think

Let me say up front that I do not object to protocols in principle. I have been responsible for the development of several protocols, both for trauma and for critical care. At their best, protocols serve as guidelines and memory aides prompting us to do the right thing to help and protect our patients. They can be powerful reminders and guides for those who don't often deal with a particular problem, or conversely, may keep those of us for whom certain critical interventions are routine from becoming complacent.

I do object to protocols that take the place of critical thinking, especially when that is coupled with an electronic medical record that forces the physician to follow a checklist. Recently this was brought home during an episode at my primary hospital.

My patient was a 59-year-old man who had under gone a laparoscopic assisted right colectomy. He was a two pack a day smoker and had some modest high blood pressure. He did well with surgery and the initial postop period. On day three however, he became hypoxic (low oxygen saturation in the blood), tachycardic (rapid heart rate) and a little confused. This was enough to trigger a 'sepsis alert".

Severe sepsis is an inflammatory response to severe infection. It is an exaggerated expression of the fever and normal inflammation that accompany an infection. It can cause a cascade of low blood pressure, fever, poor tissue perfusion and acidosis leading to organ failure and death.

The sepsis initiative is designed to improve outcomes by identifying patients with early sepsis and providing physicians with a standard set of orders to treat it. So far so good.

So when the sepsis alert triggered on my patient, I first looked at his blood pressure and temperature. Both were normal. Then I checked the trend of his oxygen saturations. They had been declining slowly for several hours before they reached a 'critical' level. Finally, I remembered the old surgical adage, 'When all else fails, examine the patient'. He was sitting up in bed, awake and alert with very little pain. He was breathing rapidly but his breath was not labored. He was not wheezing and although the breath sounds were diminished in the lower part of his chest, they improved with a cough. All signs of an early pneumonia, a common postoperative risk for a smoker. It explained his hypoxia, his rapid pulse and his brief confusion. He needed antibiotics and aggressive pulmonary toilet (coughing, deep breathing and maybe nebulizer treatments), but he was not septic.

I tried to order the appropriate treatments but the sepsis order set kept popping up and I couldn't do anything until I had checked off the boxes on the list. I didn't need blood cultures, I didn't need a serum lactate, and I didn't need blood tests or a transfer to a monitored bed. I ended up ordering a bunch of things I didn't need and then canceling the orders once the sepsis alert was satisfied.

I have been doing trauma and critical care for thirty years. I'm very familiar with the presentation and treatment of sepsis. I also understand that many physicians do not have my level of experience and training. The sepsis order set is a useful guide, but it does not replace critical thinking. The way that the electronic record has set it up, however, a physician who has actually evaluated the patient and decided that sepsis is not present can't over ride the order set. I can't help but wonder how many unnecessary tests and transfers to higher-level care are happening as a result of physicians not taking the time to do that evaluation, or not being comfortable with deviating from the order set.

I finished the orders and spoke to the patient's nurse about his status. I thought that resolved the matter. Two hours later, the nursing supervisor paged me. She asked me if I was aware that a sepsis alert had been triggered on my patient. Yes, I said, and it's been taken care of.

"Well, I noticed that you hadn't ordered blood cultures or a lactic acid level. Would you like me to put those orders in for you?"

I struggled to keep my temper, or at least remain civil. "No," I said. "I saw the patient and ordered the appropriate measures to deal with his problem."

"But the sepsis protocol is incomplete," she said, as if that was more important than my evaluation.

"He has pneumonia, not systemic sepsis."

"Patients can be septic from pneumonia," she said in a condescending tone.

"Yes they can," I agreed. "How will a lactic acid level help me take care of his pneumonia? And how will blood cultures tell me what bacteria are in his sputum?"

Dead silence. She clearly had no clue what the tests on the protocol were designed to look for, or even what the real issue with systemic sepsis was. (Hint: it's all about blood pressure and tissue perfusion)

"So you don't want these orders entered?" she finally asked.

It took all of my limited self-control to not scream, "NO you stupid idiot. I don't."

"No thank you," I managed to growl and hung up before she could say anything else.

Cynicism

The title says it all. I get like this sometimes after a week of making rounds on the trauma service and doing two or three trauma ER shifts during the same week. I have little love or hope for humanity today. It is often said that the only two certain things are death and taxes. To that I would add stupidity.

A few days ago I was watching a medical drama on TV. I shouldn't do that; it either makes me laugh or ticks me off. An earnest young character on the show made the statement that trauma happens to anyone--most trauma patients are ordinary people who get up every day and go to work and pay their bills until some random event blindsides them. HA! Most trauma patients are at best marginal participants in society and at worst drunks and drug addicts. Statistics bear this out. Trauma is disproportionately a problem of the marginalized segment of society. Alcohol is involved in more that 50% of traumas. The number of trauma patients I see who are either on chronic narcotics or psychiatric drugs approaches 80%. Trauma affects people who take risks. Not the controlled risks that skydivers and motocross racers take; the uncontrolled risk one takes when one drives at freeway speeds with a blood alcohol three times the legal limit. Either that or the risk inherent in doing something really stupid like jumping from a second floor balcony into a play pool with only three feet of water in it or trying to Evel Kneivel a dirt bike from a standing start out of the back of a pickup truck. Gravity is a bitch to those who try to cheat it.

Of the twenty plus inpatients on the trauma service today, I would classify three as 'ordinary people blindsided by a random event'. I know that is horribly cynical of me. I like to think it doesn't affect my care of them. I sincerely hope not. But I do know that I don't have a very good rapport with many of them, and in subtle ways I'm sure that does affect their care. Some of them are awfully hard to love, though.

Those of you who have read my stories know that I'm a romantic. I'm liable to cry at Hallmark commercials. And I know this cynicism is just the flip side of the same coin. It affects many of us in this business. It goes by many names--burnout, compassion fatigue, vicarious PTSD to name a few. One of the reasons I write is to try to relieve some of the feeling of futility I get sometimes. I guess if I were a true optimist, I'd say that it represents job security. People will always do stupid things and so trauma surgeons will always have plenty to do. Thank God the week is almost over and I can get back to more rewarding work, like cancer surgery.

Reprocess: Safe or Not

The latest cost saving move by my main hospital is to use 'reprocessed' laparoscopic instruments. Things like clip appliers, scissors and harmonic shears that we use to control bleeding, cut tissue and control bleeding. The manufacturers of these instruments intend for them to be used once and then thrown away.

There are reasons for this. The instruments are made of plastic and thin steel. They are robust enough for use but not for resterilization. The moving parts are small and have a lot of nooks and crannies that are hard to clean.

Nevertheless, there is a company that sees opportunity here. They take used instruments, disassemble them, clean and sterilize them, replace broken parts and them sell them at half the price of new gear. This is against the manufacturers recommendation but the company doing it claims to have reliability data that demonstrates the gear to be safe and effective. Unfortunately, there is no FDA regulation covering this process. The FDA can't or won't certify the safety of reprocessed gear, nor will they restrict it.

Despite company and hospital claims, my personal experience with this stuff has not been good. At one of the hospitals where I work, all they provide is reprocessed gear. In the course of three days I had three separate harmonic shear fail during surgery, had a clip applier lock on a blood vessel forcing me to tear the vessel in order to remove the device, and had a scissors fall apart during use. I know anecdotal experience is not scientific, but I personally will not use reprocessed gear unless compelled to do so.

As yet, my main hospital is not forcing surgeons to use this stuff, but the hospital is part of a big system and they are under pressure to use the gear. I am currently department chair and refuse to allow it. That may be an empty gesture, since I don't control purchasing and can't really keep the gear out if the hospital forces us to use it. All I can do is resign in protest.

My problem is threefold: First, I have not seen any independent reliability data that shows reprocessed gear is at least as safe as new. It may exist, but all I've seen is information provided by the reprocessing company, not exactly objective. To be fair, the opposition data comes from the manufacturer of the new gear and can't be trusted either. To date I have seen no independent assessment of the gear. Second, the reprocessing company says they only reprocess an instrument once, not repeatedly. But they depend on the hospital to throw the item away so it doesn't get back into the reprocess bin. There is no tag or identifying label on the instrument to make sure it doesn't happen. If ALL your gear is reprocessed, you just throw it away at the end of the case, but if you mix new with reprocessed there is the potential for error. As yet there is no identifier for the reprocessed gear. Finally there is the liability issue. I'm being asked to use a device in a way that the manufacturer of that device strongly recommends against. Who is going to indemnify me for that. I don't relish standing up in court and saying 'Yes I knew that the manufacturer recommends against reusing this equipment, but I went ahead and did it anyway and the patient had a bad outcome as a result'.

 Like I said, I may not be able to keep this stuff out of my operating room. But if given the choice, I won't use it. And I'm advising the surgeons in my department to destroy every single use instrument on their surgical fields once they are done with it.

Blood Thinners From Hell

There is a major ad campaign on the media right now pushing anticoagulant drugs that are alternatives to warfarin for the prevention of stroke in A-fib. For my non-medical friends, A-fib is Atrial Fibrillation, a heart condition where the upper chambers of the heart, the atria, don't contract properly but just quiver in a disjointed way. It's usually due to ischemic heart disease that affects the normal pacemaker cells of the heart. The lack of contraction causes blood to pool and stagnate in the atria and clots can form. They may then break up and travel to the brain causing a stroke. In order to prevent this, patients are put on anticoagulants, commonly known as blood thinners, to reduce this clotting tendency and reduce the risk of stroke.

For years, the standard drug for this purpose was warfarin (brand name Coumadin). Warfarin blocks the use of vitamin K by the liver in the manufacture of certain clotting factors, proteins needed to make blood clot. If the level of those K dependent factors is reduced, the blood doesn't clot as readily and the risk of stroke is reduced.

Warfarin is not an easy drug to use. Dosing is highly individual and depends more on the efficiency of the enzyme system in the liver than on body weight or age. The proper dose can vary between individuals and even over time in the same individual. It needs regular monitoring with a blood test and often the dose needs to be adjusted.

Warfarin is also relatively easy to reverse. High doses of vitamin K will do it over a couple of days. Fresh Frozen Plasma (FFP, a blood component) will do it within hours. Prothrombin Complex Concentrate (PCC, a concentrate one of the K factors made by recombinant DNA genetics from bacteria) will do it in minutes, but costs thousands of dollars per milligram.

Patients don't like warfarin because of the dosing issues and the need for regular blood draws, so there was an incentive to come up with products that would work as well and not need monitoring. These are now being pushed through aggressive direct marketing on television and other media. They include such products as Rivaroxaban and Apixaban, Dabigatran, and Clopidogrel. (I am using the generic rather than the trade names to reduce the risk of a liability suit here). All will reduce the stroke risk, similar to warfarin, but don't need constant monitoring. Some even claim to have a lower risk of bleeding complications than warfarin (a distortion that I will address shortly).

So what's wrong with these new drugs? Aside from the questionable practice of direct marketing of prescription drugs in general? The big issue for surgeons is that they can't be reversed. Surgeons hate all anticoagulants. They are antithetical to our basic method of treatment. I can't do surgery on a patient who won't stop bleeding when I make an incision. Even more troublesome is the trauma patient on anticoagulants who has uncontrolled bleeding before I even get involved.

Warfarin is difficult to use and has a higher risk of SPONTANEOUS bleeding than the newer agents, but at least I can turn it off in an emergency. Spontaneous bleeding does occur with all of these agents. That is, bleeding, usually into large muscles, but occasionally into the brain, that is not related to any trauma or obvious cause. It isn't terribly common but is not rare. The makers or Apixaban claim their drug has a lower bleeding complication rate than warfarin, which is true if you only look at spontaneous bleeding.

The picture is very different if you look at bleeding after trauma. The newer agents have a much higher risk of bleeding related complications, brain injury and transfusion requirement than warfarin. This is to be expected, since, unlike warfarin, they can't be reversed.

A frequent scenario in the trauma center is the ground-level fall in an elderly patient. These can cause fractures and brain hemorrhage in any frail older patient. In those on anticoagulants, the risk of brain bleeding is at least an order of magnitude higher. With warfarin, a serious brain bleed can be shut down within minutes with PCC's. Clopidigrel takes 5 days to reverse on its own. Giving platelets and clotting factors doesn't help until the at least half of the therapeutic dose clears the system. Dabigatran goes away in two days, but responds to nothing until then. Rivaoxaban and Apixaban take two days to clear according to the manufacturers. Personal experience suggests it's more like five. Meanwhile, the patient may continue to bleed at a rate from slow oozing to a continuous hemorrhage. This can be hard enough to deal with in an open abdomen or limb fracture. In the closed space of the skull, it can be the difference between recovery and death.

So far all I have said is documented in peer reviewed studies and clinical experience. What I will now say is purely opinion. I think it was highly, almost criminally, irresponsible of both the FDA and the manufacturers of these drugs to allow their release without adequate reversal agents. The evidence for their safety and efficacy is based on healthy volunteer studies and limited real world clinical studies that DROPPED any patient who suffered trauma or had emergency surgery during the study period. So their data on safety is based only on the ideal scenario of an uneventful course of treatment with no spontaneous bleeding. Further, spontaneous bleeding with warfarin is only higher when patients with inadequate monitoring are considered. If the blood tests are done appropriately, the risk is low.

The manufacturers of these drugs distorted the data on surgery or trauma in patients taking these medications and glossed over the relative risk of things like falls and head injury. Falls and head injuries are significantly higher in the elderly than in people under the age of 65. And who is most likely to need these drugs? Hint: It isn't people under 65.

While it is too late to completely withdraw these medications without a new ruling by the FDA, I would caution anyone facing the decision on what anticoagulant to use to consider more than just convenience. For anyone taking ANY anticoagulants I would recommend avoiding bicycles, motorcycles, climbing ladders more than two steps high, or any sort of contact sport. A simple fall, even with a helmet can result in a life-threatening brain bleed. Be careful with power tools, knives, and sharp implements of all kinds. I'm not advocating being completely homebound and wrapping yourself in cotton balls, but always be aware that even minor injuries carry the risk of major bleeding. And with the new drugs, my colleagues and I may have no way to stop the hemorrhage.

Gun Control and the Real World

A high school acquaintance and Facebook friend who regularly comments on Huffington Post recently posted a heartfelt essay on gun violence. I responded in my usual fashion with statistics and legal citations. Others responded and even suggested I view a YouTube video of people talking about the personal effect of the violent deaths of their loved ones. As if I didn't 'get it'.

I realize that my initial response was wrong. The essay wasn't about real solutions to gun violence. It was an appeal to emotion, to a common sense idea that if the gun were taken out of the equation, the personal confrontations that had resulted in a death would have been less lethal. The idea is indisputable – guns escalate the potential lethality of any situation.

And believe me, I 'get it' when it comes to the personal devastation of a violent death. I'm the guy who has to tell a family that the gunshot wound their loved one inflicted on themselves was fatal and that they are gone forever. I'm the one who has to tell the parents of a 16 year old that his brain has no reasonable hope of recovery and ask if they've considered organ donation. I'm the one who is up to his elbows in someone else's blood at two in the morning trying to staunch the flood from a severed aorta. I am an intimate participant in our nation's dance of violence and death.

I am also a realist. 'What if the gun weren't there' is little more than wishful thinking if it doesn't lead to a solution. The only real solution to the impulsive use of a gun in a confrontation or in a suicide is to remove guns from the general population. And that is simply unrealistic in this country, at this time in history. Blame whomever you like. I don't care. There is simply no way that guns will go away any time soon. Bromides about mental health screening and background checks are feel-good measures. They will likely stop some really bad or crazy people from acquiring a gun, but that is a tiny minority of the people who use guns on their fellow humans. Most are regular people who succumb to a moment of rage or bad judgment or despair that is then made tragic by the easy access to a deadly weapon.

I don't offer a solution because I don't believe there is one; at least not one that is palatable to most people. Gun control? Sure. Gun confiscation on a national scale? Um, wait a minute. And make no mistake, in order to stop all impulsive acts of gun violence, that's what it would take. If there is a solution, it will come through hard-bitten realism and careful analysis of a public health problem. Not through emotional appeals to a national conscience that is fleeting and abdicates it's responsibility to nameless government functionaries.

Patient's satisfaction

Patient's satisfaction is one of the new buzzwords in our current ongoing struggle with the American medical care system. Physicians and hospitals are rated on patient satisfaction surveys and our reimbursement through Medicare is intimately tied to these ratings. But what does patient satisfaction really mean? More importantly how accurate are the measures that are being used to determine patient satisfaction? The current survey, which is standardized and distributed to all patient's leaving the hospital, is not individualized for each physician that the patient saw during her hospital stay. Rather an aggregate score is assigned to all of the physicians who were involved in the patient's care. The patient simply answers a scaled questionnaire on how well the doctor listened to you, how well the doctor treated you with respect, and how well the doctor explained your medical problems and procedures. The doctor in question however is not identified. This means that if several doctors were involved in the patient's care, the one that was the most memorable to the patient will be the one that is rated. He or she may be memorable because they were particularly good, or particularly bad. Anyone else involved in that care is tarred with the same brush.

I was recently reminded of the vagaries of patient satisfaction when I saw a patient in my office in follow up. This was a woman who had had a particularly complex surgical problem, and had a very difficult and demanding operation. She was not in the best of health and was a poor candidate for the surgery in the first place. I was very proud of my efforts, since the surgery was exceedingly difficult but went very well. Furthermore her postoperative care was top-notch and she had no significant complications. When I saw her in my office however she was quite angry and upset. She swore she would never again go back to that hospital, and thought that it was one of the worst experiences of her life. I was taken aback. I had put forth extra effort doing a complex bit of surgery and then taking care of a very sick woman and was expecting a modicum of gratitude or at least appreciation. I had spent a good deal of time prior to the surgery describing its complexity, and informing her of the very high-risk nature of the procedure.

    I dug a little deeper to try to discover the source of her anger. It turned out that she had multiple complaints about the physical plant of the hospital, the cleanliness of her bathroom, the quality of the food, and the promptness of the nursing staff in dealing with her requests and demands. These are all things that I consider peripheral to her care but to her were quite central to it.

    I was reminded of the importance of patient perception after a recent airplane trip. I flew from Phoenix to San Jose for a training course. The flight itself was uneventful other than some high altitude turbulence. We took off and landed safely and arrived on time. I was nevertheless somewhat unhappy at the end of the flight because there had been a long delay in boarding, I was forced to sit in a middle seat rather than an aisle seat, and they were out of my choice of beverage. Completely lost on me was the fact that we had just flown hundreds of miles at 35,000 feet where the outside temperature was 50°below zero and there was not enough oxygen to sustain life. We had passed through an area of turbulence with very little incident and had landed safely and on time. I was completely discounting the skill and training of the pilot, the people who maintain the aircraft, and the air traffic controller who guided us safely to our destination. These are all very complex interactions with involving multiple people all of whom have highly skilled jobs to do. For me a safe flight and on time arrival was simply the expectation. My expectations were not met with respect to boarding, seating, and my beverage choice. I'm sure that to the flight crew and pilot, these are all things that were quite peripheral to a safe flight, and my complaining about them now seems petty.

    It may not be fair, but we need to remember that peoples' experience is based on a point of view, and not necessarily on the complexity of the interaction going on around them. My patient was upset about things that directly affected her and her comfort. It was her expectation that she would have a safe and successful surgery and that the people caring for her would do their jobs properly. Where her expectations were not met, there was certainly room for improvement, but in the overall importance of her hospital stay and they were relatively minor. To her, however, they were the defining aspects of her experience.

Anger Management

"'Anyone can become angry – that's easy. But to be angry with the right person, to the right degree, at the right time, for the right purpose, and in the right way – this is not easy' ". Aristotle

This is a lesson that I have struggled to learn for more that thirty years. I am better than I used to be, but still have a short fuse. There was a time when, as a patient once put it, I was the 'Bobby Knight of the operating room'. I didn't consider it a compliment then and don't now. Temper tantrums in the OR are destructive to moral and disrupt the flow of an operation. Yelling at the staff doesn't make them work harder or smarter; it just makes them dislike working with you. I still get loud, curse and fume, but direct it mainly at myself. I studiously avoid blaming my scrub nurse, tech, or first assistant. The reason a case isn't going well is seldom their fault in any event. As a mentor once said, "If the operation is hard, you're doing something wrong." The flow and pace of the surgery is my responsibility, not theirs.

Once my patient is admitted to an inpatient floor, the situation is different. I'm still responsible for the care, but no longer in control. I can't sit at the bedside 24 hours a day and watch over a patient.

So when my orders get screwed up or when the care is indifferent of incompetent I look to the nurse caring for the patient to take responsibility for the problem. When this doesn't happen, I need to remember Aristotle's advice. The right person – not the day nurse who has no control over the previous night's actions; the right degree (sometimes I go overboard); and especially the right purpose – correcting the problem and making sure I'm kept informed in the future.

I once overheard a nurse I knew well talking to a new hire. He said, "Don't worry about calling Dr. Davis in the middle of the night. Just make sure you have your shit together before you do." That I took as a complement.

Complications

Yesterday I readmitted two patients to the hospital with surgical complications. One was a man who had a colon resection six weeks ago. He has had the 'dwindles' since discharge. He's lost weight, has no energy and no appetite. A CBC done yesterday showed his white blood cell count was elevated and a metabolic panel shows impending renal failure. I suspect he has an intrabdominal abscess despite the fact that he has no fever.

The second patient is three weeks out from a complex incisional hernia repair that involved reconstruction of her entire abdominal wall with placement of a large sheet of surgical mesh under the muscle layers. She is a morbidly obese diabetic and has developed a wound infection. If the infection reaches the mesh, I'll have to remove it, undoing her entire repair.

Complications are a fact of life in surgery. No matter how good a surgeon you are, no matter how carefully you manage patients, something will go wrong once in a while. As my Chief was fond of saying, "If you do big surgery, you get big complications." Intellectually I know this. But days like yesterday try my soul.

The first thing I ask myself when a patient has a complication after surgery is, "What did I do wrong?" Did I make a technical error? Did I miss some critical sign or lab value? I'm not comfortable until I've looked for those things, and even then feel that I must have missed something. This is the default mode for most surgeons I know. That type of thinking is built into our training. The ritual of the Morbidity and Mortality conference emphasizes taking responsibility for everything that happens to your patient. Only then can your peers grant you absolution for your mistakes. I suspect most of us tend to be hyper-responsible pessimists at heart or we wouldn't have selected this career in the first place.

The Wise Woman (my wife) tells me that taking responsibility for things I can't control is arrogant, a form of narcissism that imagines that I am able to control the forces of random chance. I understand her point and accept it. My difficulty is separating those things I can control from those I can't.

Both of these people had issues before surgery, and that's another truth I must concede. Trauma is a high-risk practice but even my general surgery practice tends toward the high risk/low reward type of procedures. I'm not sure if that's a complement to my surgical skill or just because I'm willing to operate on people whom others have turned down. These people are more likely to have postoperative problems that the healthy thirty-year-old gallbladder patient. So perhaps the failing isn't in technical skill or in postop care but rather in judgment and patient selection.

Whatever the root cause of this particular round of surgical complications, I'm still the one who has to clean up my own mess. That is a responsibility any surgeon must accept before he places a knife on the patients skin. Acknowledging the responsibility doesn't make it any easier to face my patients on rounds in the morning, but at least it helps me sleep at night.

I Am Not A Patient Advocate

People have commented on some of my posts, expressing appreciation for my 'patient advocacy'. I hate that term. Let's get something straight. I am not a patient advocate. Patient advocates are nurses and social workers with a Mother Teresa complex who see their mission as protecting the patient from evil uncaring doctors who would subject them to unnecessary pain and indignity. I have little tolerance for such people. If I am anything, I am an honest craftsman.

When a patient comes to my office seeking surgical care, I am making a pact with them, a contract if you will. I pledge my honor as a surgeon, as an honest man, that I will do the right thing for them. The right operation for the right reason at the right time. I will be conscientious in the operating room and will do my utmost to give them a smooth and uneventful recovery. To the extent that I do these things, my patient will do well and recover. If there is a complication, the first question I ask is "What did I do wrong?"

Note that in all of that, the real issue is my personal duty and integrity. If I do all those things right, the patient will recover and do well. But in the end, it's not about the patient – it's about the integrity of the WORK. The patient's recovery is a happy side effect. It is the work that is the real motivation.

My personal integrity is at stake each time I go to the operating room. I have pledged to that patient to do my best. I don't want to know them as people, I don't have to like them or understand them. Sometimes it's better if I don't. I treat the gangbanger with the gunshot wound to the abdomen with the same attention to detail that I bring to the colon resection on the 70-year-old grandmother who bakes cookies for all the neighborhood kids. In the operating room, NONE OF THAT MATTERS. What matters is the skill I bring to my craft.

The highest complement anyone can pay me isn't to say, " He's a good surgeon." Or "He looks out for his patients." The true recognition of what I'm about is, "He does what he says he'll do."

Medicare Wonderland

She is 77 years old, a bit frail, and has a recurrent breast cancer 15 years after lumpectomy and radiation in the same breast. Her only option is a mastectomy. She lives alone and has no family in the area. Most of her friends are snowbirds – they leave Arizona for the summer and return when the weather gets cold up north. She has had a total hip and total knee replacement and isn't too concerned about the mastectomy, since she recovered reasonably well after those procedures.

The problem is that mastectomy is now considered an outpatient procedure by CMS, the agency that makes the rules for Medicare. That means that in order to admit her to the hospital as an inpatient, I have to document 'medical necessity'. Being old and frail isn't considered 'medical necessity'.

I do her surgery and write orders in the recovery room for Observation Status. This is a loophole that lets me put her in a hospital bed for 23hrs to see if there is a medical reason to require admission. It's intended for ER patients with things like chest pain of uncertain origin, shortness of breath, fevers, etc. Surgeons have learned that we can use this status to give patients time to recover from anesthesia and regroup before going home. The alternative is to discharge directly from the recovery room within an hour or so of surgery.

I am called almost immediately by a Case Manager wanting to know what my diagnosis is that requires Observation. My stock response is pain control – the patient is receiving intravenous narcotics. It's a bit of a cheat since they are not awake enough to take pills, but both the hospital and CMS have winked at that for years. Not anymore, apparently. Fortunately, her oxygen saturation is a bit low in the recovery room, giving me another excuse to admit her.

By the next morning, she is taking a diet, her pain is controlled and her oxygen is normal. She is still weak, however, and needs two nurses to get her out of bed. I write to convert her to an inpatient admission, since she clearly can't go home.

Again the Case Manager calls. Her weakness isn't considered an admission criterion. I get a little snarky and ask the Case Manager if she is willing to take my patient home and care for her, but that doesn't really help. Now she's hostile and tells me I can extend the Observation and get a Physical Therapy evaluation. It's not what I want, but at least it buys another day. By Friday morning, my patient is still weak, but has managed to walk 'community distance' (50ft) with PT and is again 'ready for discharge'.

I am reluctant to send her home. By objective criteria, she's ready; but looking at her, I am afraid she's at risk for falling, she can't prepare her own meals, and she won't cooperate with the nurses in learning to manage her drain. None of which buy her an admission. I talk to the Social Worker and we set up a Home Health visit for one drain care visit and a home safety evaluation. She goes home in the early afternoon.

Through this whole process, my hands have been tied by Medicare rules. I can't do what I consider the right thing and admit the patient for a few days. I can write the orders, but Medicare will refuse payment of the hospital charges. I can lie about her condition, I can falsify or exaggerate her problems, but there are others charting on her record that would reveal the inconsistency and I'd be up on a fraud charge. So I reluctantly send her home.

She lasts 18hrs. Then she falls at home, can't get up, and pulls her drain out in the process. Fortunately she has one of those Medic Alert pendants and calls an ambulance. I see her in the ER an hour or so later. Other than the drain being out prematurely, she is unhurt. Her wound is fine, she has a small bruise on her knee and her chin, but that's all. I again write admission orders. Surely she has just demonstrated that she is unsafe to be home alone. I don't even get to sign the order before the Case Manager is on my back again. Falling without injury isn't an admission criterion. I can put her in Observation again, but that's all.

I lose my temper and tell the Case Manager where to put her admission criteria (Hint: the sun doesn't shine on the place I suggest) and storm out of the ER. Before I get to my car, the hospital's Medical Officer is paging me. All hospitals have a Medical Officer, a paid lackey who nominally provides a clinical voice to advise the administration on good care and resolve conflict between physicians. In reality, they have sold out and enforce the administration's line of BS. He first takes me to task for losing my temper with the Case Manager. In this he is right and I promise to apologize to her right away.

Then he starts on a long winded explanation of CMS Medicare rules and admission criteria. I tell him I'm well aware of the documentation needed, but unfortunately, my patient meets none of the criteria. What she really needs is a Skilled Nursing Facility for a few days. But here's the catch – in order for Medicare to pay any of the cost of a SNF, the patient has to have three continuous days of hospitalization. The Observation days DON'T COUNT! Which is why I have been pushing for admission from day one. The SMO repeats the criteria for admission and then tells me that if I don't change my admission order I'll be committing Medicare Fraud. The shouting match that ensues erases any trace of cooperation.

In that, I am at fault. I lost my temper and alienated the SMO and the Case Manager. It wouldn't have changed anything had I been more polite, but the discussion would have been more pleasant. What my patient needs is irrelevant to the bureaucracy. All I can do is keep finding excuses to keep her in Observation and hope she gets strong enough to be safe at home. In the end, I send her home again with another Home Health referral.

There's a lesson here for all those who think that a single payer system will solve all of our healthcare problems. Medicare is defacto a single payer system for those over 65. There is no alternative other than paying out of pocket. The rules under which we treat Medicare patient are set by CMS and are often arbitrary and capricious. The emphasis is on cost containment, not clinical effectiveness. This is clear from such stupidity as the three day inpatient rule cited above; from the refusal to pay for screening tests recommended by the American College of Cardiology (due to cost issues); from the SCIP surgical protocol which has been shown in a half dozen studies to be at best irrelevant and yet CMS requires a 98% compliance with it for all surgical patients. The problem is less about who pays than it is about who decides what gets paid for.

But wait, some say, aren't insurance companies even worse about paying for care? Don't we hear about that all the time in the media? In fact, insurers are generally much better at covering clinically indicated care than CMS. We hear about the egregious exceptions, about the transplants denied or the experimental but lifesaving therapy that isn't covered. But Medicare doesn't cover that stuff either. And in my experience, if there is truly a valid clinical reason for a test or operation, I can talk to the insurance company's medical advisor and lay out my case to him or her. Most of the time, the service is approved. In CMS, there is no one to talk to, no appeal other than to faceless and nameless bureaucrats who have no responsibility to individual patients, only to their budgets.

Vocabulary Matters

We had a speaker at our regular Wednesday trauma meeting today, some administrator who was telling us about new staffing policies for the hospital and how many nurses we'd be losing from the trauma service. She went on and on about the 'negative impact of declining reimbursement' and the 'projected impact of attrition on staff levels' and the 'impact of Obamacare on the ER population' until I wanted to scream. The information was important since it affects the way we will plan for our trauma shifts, but I wanted to shake her and shout, "The word you want is AFFECT." IMPACT is a physics term.

If I hit you in the nose with a baseball bat, you've been 'impacted'. If funding for your favorite project is cut you've been 'affected'. Somewhere along the way, the bean counters and middle managers decided that using 'impact' made their inherently boring talks sexy and more interesting. It's become such a cliché that no one notices anymore; no one except curmudgeons like me. Rant finished.

Age and the Trauma Surgeon, Part 2

I'm facing another Saturday trauma shift and feeling every bit my age. Trauma on a Saturday usually means no sleep and a steady stream of business. Back in the old days, when I was in my thirties, I could operate for 24 hours straight, catch a few hours of sleep and get up refreshed and do it again. Now it takes me a couple of days to recover from one of those marathon sessions.

My performance in the operating room isn't affected. A number of studies have confirmed what every surgeon knows from personal experience: fatigue doesn't significantly affect performance in surgery. And in the operating room, age and cunning always trump youth and enthusiasm. Older surgeons retain their edge over younger ones even when fatigued. There's tremendous advantage in 'been there, done that'. When the unexpected happens, the older surgeon spends less time thinking about his next move. He's learned the hard way how to do things his mentors never taught him.

It's after the drapes come off and the dressings go on and you have to write orders and notes and talk to the family that there is an advantage to the resiliency of youth. You can feel the energy drain away like someone pulled the plug. Error creeps in when you have to decide on medications and dosages and how to phrase a delicate question.

I tend to get short tempered and cranky. (Those who know me will now ask, "And how is that different from when you're well rested", so maybe I should say MORE cranky than usual). I have to think harder to remember names and dates and medications. And the after effects last longer these days.

So, I expect I'll be up all night tomorrow night and be pretty much a zombie even when I'm awake all day Sunday. It's hard on those around me. My wife is a surgical nurse practitioner and knows first hand the rigors of the job. She understands. My autistic son is now almost an adult and even he knows that Dad needs to nap, but he only has the weekend to spend time with me and it's hard for him. And even though I try to be polite to others, my tolerance for stupidity and frustration is low and I'm liable to say things I'll later regret.

So how much longer will I continue this work? I don't know. Despite the fatigue and frustration, there's nothing else like it. Trauma is like combat - often boring, but at times exciting beyond words and above all, addictive.

## Afterward

This is not my first book. I have written several novels that are currently available through Amazon as both print and e-books. This book grew out of a personal journey as well as a writing project. One cannot recall and relive these experiences without being touched anew by the emotions they evoked.

I wish to thank all of my colleagues – surgeons, mentors, nurses and technicians – without whose support, teaching, and fine everyday work I would not be able to do what I do. Surgery is a team sport played by individuals and often the team does not get the recognition it deserves.

Thank you also to Terri L Smith for her provocative and insightful comments on the manuscript.

To all my friends and contacts, colleagues and supporters who have watched this work evolve from a series of on-line rants to a finished work, I have enjoyed and learned from your comments and feedback.

Finally, to my wife, Michele, who has been my partner, my editor, my sounding board, and the love of my life for over thirty years, thank you for your patience and strength. I love you.

Bruce Davis, MD
February 2015

Made in the USA
San Bernardino, CA
24 February 2015